PARABLES
IN THE NIGHT SEASONS
UNDERSTANDING YOUR DREAMS

Joy Parrott

Parables in the Night Seasons, Understanding Your Dreams
Copyright © 2002 by Joy Parrott
All rights reserved.
Fifth Printing, September 2006

All Scripture quotations, unless otherwise indicated, are taken from
the New King James Version. Copyright © by Thomas Nelson, Inc.

Published by Glory Publications
Joy Parrott Ministries
35855 57th Ave. So
Auburn, WA 98001
(253) 288-0574
www.joyparrott.com

ISBN 0-9727720-0-6

Cover Picture Copyright © 2002
Robert Bartow. Used with Permission.
Cover Design by Paul Jones

Dedication

This book is dedicated to Jesse Parrott, my husband who has believed in me and supported me throughout all the endeavors that I have put my hands and heart to. He has always pulled forth the God potential within me and for that I am eternally grateful. Thank you for your endless support and self sacrificing love. I love you!

My children, who are always ready to roll up their sleeves and get their hands in to help me with the ministry. I love and appreciate you!

Wayne Beckman, my mother's husband, who is like a father to me. He has loved me as his own and has taught me to know the love of our heavenly Father through his unconditional love and support. I love you dearly.

Char Beckman, my mother, who thinks I'm perfect! (Well almost!) With that kind of confidence in me, how can I fail! I love you mom!

Acknowledgements

My thanks and gratitude to all of the following people…

- Kristy Nelson, my dream partner who shared and listened to endless dreams and encouraged me concerning my gifting in the interpretations of dreams. Thank you for overlooking those times when I really missed it! I love you!
- Linda Blaylock, who has more faith in me than I do myself! Thank you for your amazing love, self sacrificing support and encouragement. I could not have done it without you! And to her husband Bob who has made me feel like part of his family. Thank you for your encouragement and love and for loaning your wife to me when ministry calls!
- Kari Browning, who took a risk by inviting me to speak on dreams at her Training Center. Thank you for taking the risk, for believing in me, and encouraging me to go for the gold (and diamonds)! I appreciate your friendship and love you dearly. And to her husband Mike, thank you for putting up with the dream lady!
- Greg Wilkinson, who helped me to believe I could actually write! But only after he painstakingly edited my work and made this book palatable to the reader. I appreciate you and all your help. And to his wife Vernie, who interceded on behalf of this book, thank you! Your support and prayers mean more than you can imagine.

- Jeri Woods who saw the anointing in my life and pushed me to share my gifting and talents with the body of Christ. I thank you for all the mentoring and practical experience you gave me.
- Dawn Morgan who encouraged me in the beginning stages of my ministry. Thank you.
- Adrienne Hickey who transposed my tapes so that I could get my thoughts on paper. Thank you, you truly were a Godsend!
- Finally and most importantly my Heavenly Father who is my best friend, counselor, encourager and comforter. This is His book and to Him I give all the glory, honor and praise!

Contents

PART II: WHERE DO YOUR DREAMS COME FROM?

Foreword

Parables in the Night Seasons, subtitled *Understanding Your Dreams*, is the best, most thoroughly biblical book on the subject I have ever read, bar none, including my own chapters on dreams and visions! Joy combines practical common sense and high spirituality, deep insights and simple humility, in a teaching so clear and profound that I intend to make the book required reading for all of our prayer counselors in all our Elijah Houses, national and international, and in all our affiliates.

Parrott parrots no one else - forgive the too obvious pun. Her insights are unique, while at the same moment consonant with the many dreamers of the Bible whom she quotes so deftly. Those who would learn to make sense of the often mysterious and confusing language of the world of dreams will find solid sign posts here that lead to growth in clear comprehension. Chapters Six, Seven and Eight, "Watchman Dreams," "Pizza Dreams," and "Double Dreams," are so valuable as alone to be worth more than the price of purchase and study. I can hardly wait for the sequel, *Watchman, Watchman, What of the Night?*

This is that time in history in which God is raising His prophets for His end-time purposes. "If a *prophet or a dreamer of dreams* arises among you...(Deuteronomy 13:1)," makes it unequivocal that the Lord regards prophets and dreamers as one and the same. Unfortunately, the Body of Christ, for the most part, has not yet grasped that. It is imperative that at least His prophets and hopefully the entire Body, come to comprehend how important this aspect of prophets' equipment actually is, and that all His prophets become adepts both in having their own dreams and in interpreting theirs and those of others. **One**

**cannot read *Parables in the Night Seasons* without awakening
to the need to go to sleep and dream.** If for that reason alone,
the book is timely and a valuable gift from the Lord for this time
especially.

Though filled with examples and stories, *Parables...* is not
froth, to be enjoyed and put down only to pick up the next
exciting book. It ought to become a manual for study in all the
Lord's various "green trees" (training places for beginning
prophets). It will become so in our Elijah House schools.
"*Parables...* is meant to be put to work. Its pages call us from
ho-hum acceptance of our dreams into intercessory labor and
warfare for our Lord. The Church cries out for watchmen to
arise. Tragedies can be prevented. Blessings can be prayed in,
lest His messenger angels languish on the way, inhibited by the
"princes of Persia" that need to be defeated. God wants listening
ears, and He often prefers to speak to us through the medium of
dream language. It behooves us therefore to study to be
workmen that need not to be ashamed – or to miss the fervent
callings of the Lord.

I pray God may prosper both the sales and the effects of
Parables in the Night Seasons, lest the night come when no man
can work - or dream. May the Day of the Lord arise with healing
in its wings (Malachi 4:1-3) - because we have learned to dream
in the night!

John Loren Sandford
Co-Founder, Elijah House, Inc.

PART I:

LAYING A FOUNDATION

Chapter 1

Dreams

Dreams...do they come from some fantasy world made up in our minds, or could there be something more to them? I have found the world of dreams to be very complex in nature. Being a dreamer all my life, I had never considered my dreams to be anything more than my vivid imagination or a dream that erupted from eating pizza the night before! I was well into my Christian walk before my spiritual eyes became opened to the fact that God has spoken to His people through dreams in times past. As I began to explore the area of dreams through the scriptures, I came to recognize that not only did God speak in dreams to His people of old, but that He still speaks to His people in dreams today! It was from this revelation that my life has been forever changed.

Are Dreams Scriptural?

When a person matures in his Christian walk, he recognizes the need to have a scriptural foundation for his life. After newly discovering that the Word of God had actual accounts of dreams, I knew that as a dreamer I needed to know whatever I could concerning them. I had such a desire and hunger to know more about this subject and whether God might be speaking to me in the night seasons. Could I have been missing God speaking to me all these years? This was a question that I could not let go of. It has always been my desire to fellowship and communicate with my Lord, and if this was one of the ways that He was speaking, then I knew I would need to have understanding.

It wasn't easy for me once I started searching for information on this topic. As my search began, I ran into very little material on this subject, and the little I did find just didn't "sit right" in my spirit. Much of it appeared to come from the angle of what I would call New Age. There just wasn't much on the area of dreams that appeared biblical to me. It was at this point that I had come to realize the only place I would be able to find my answers to the questions I had about dreams was from God. After all, He is our creator and what better source could there be? If I were to have any scriptural understanding at all concerning the area of dreams, I would need to find my answers through the Word of God. I asked the Holy Spirit to be my teacher and it is with the foundation of scripture that I present to you my understanding in the area of dreams.

> *For **God may speak in one way, or in another**, yet man does not perceive it. **In a dream**, in a vision of the night, when deep sleep falls upon men while slumbering on their beds, then He opens the ears of men and seals their instruction. In order to turn man from his deed, and conceal pride from man, He keeps back his soul from the pit, and his life from perishing by the sword* (Job 33:14-19).

Here Job is saying that God may speak in one way or another, yet man does not perceive it. He goes on to say…"In a dream, in a vision of the night." This is how it was for me, and many others just like me. I did not perceive that God could be speaking to me through my dreams. It never even crossed my mind. As a young child I would remember some of my dreams, and although they seemed very real to me, they didn't make much sense. Even well into my adulthood as I dreamed, I would not understand them. It wasn't until God had awakened my spirit to the area of dreams that I was finally able to receive some understanding concerning them. I knew that God speaks in a variety of ways, but I never would have believed that dreams are one of those ways if the Holy Spirit had not revealed it to me.

Numbers 12:6 says,

> *Then He said, "Hear now My words: If there is a prophet among you, I, the Lord, make Myself known to him in a vision; I speak to him in a dream."*

As we see from this scripture, God can make Himself known to us through a vision or a dream. Is God only speaking to His prophets in this way? No! Joel 2:28-29 says,

> *" And it shall come to pass afterward that I will pour out My Spirit on all flesh; your sons and your daughters shall prophesy, your old men shall dream dreams, your young men shall see visions. And also on My menservants and My maidservants I will pour out my Spirit in those days."*

Looking at this scripture, one might conclude that you must be an old man in order to receive dreams, but this is not so. God is indicating in this scripture that whether you are young or old, male or female, He is pouring out His Spirit and we are going to receive the benefits of it through prophesy, dreams and visions. God is pouring out His spirit on "all flesh." Even your children will dream dreams!

What is the Difference between a Dream and a Vision?

Many people have asked me, "What is the difference between a vision and a dream?" Strong's Exhaustive Concordance says that the Hebrew meaning for vision is "a sight; a dream; an oracle or revelation, especially the kind that comes through sight." It means "to gaze upon, to dream." The Hebrew meaning for dream is "vision of the night; dream." As we can see from these meanings, both a vision and a dream are of the same nature, yet one occurs while you sleep.

> *In the first year of Belshazzar king of Babylon, Daniel **had a dream** and visions of his head while on his bed. Then he **wrote down the dream**, telling the main facts. Daniel spoke, saying, "**I saw in my vision by night**, and behold, the four winds of heaven were stirring up the Great Sea"* (Daniel 7:1,2).

Here we see Daniel saying "he saw in his vision by night," yet he also refers to it as being a dream when he says, "he wrote down the dream."

> *"Now a word was secretly brought to me, and my ear received a whisper of it. In disquieting thoughts from the visions of the night, **when deep sleep falls on men**"* *(Job 4:12,13).*

Again, we see that the writer is referring to a dream as a vision of the night when we are in deep sleep. Whether you call it a dream or a vision of the night, it is the same. It is like an American talking about the evening meal: some immediately think of dinnertime, and others think of suppertime. Although these are different words, they have the same meaning. Whether you call it a dream or a vision of the night, they are one and the same. Does this make one better than the other? No, no more than dinnertime is any better than suppertime.

Are Dreams for Today?

God has always used dreams to communicate with His people. We find the first recorded dream in Genesis 20 and continue to find dreams recorded throughout the Old Testament and well into the New Testament. Some people will say that divine dreams passed away when Jesus left the earth, but this is not so. We are going to see that the great apostle Paul was also a dreamer. (I remember when I stumbled upon this revelation how excited I became — to think that Paul was a dreamer just like me!) If God was speaking to the Old Testament people and continued on through the New Testament people, then He is still speaking to us today!

> "*Jesus Christ is the same yesterday, today and forever*" (Hebrews 13:8).

> "*For I am the Lord, I do not change*" (Malachi 3:6).

If Jesus is the same and He does not change, then dreams are still for today!

Who Does God Speak To?

God speaks to both the righteous and the unrighteous (that is, those who are in right standing with God and those who are not). Some of the righteous people that God spoke to in dreams from the Old Testament are Jacob (Gen. 28:12-16), Joseph (Gen. 37:5-11), Solomon (I Kings 3:5-15) and Daniel. We can also see from the New Testament that God spoke to His people through dreams, such as to Joseph, husband of Mary (Matt. 1:20-24;2:13-15;19-21), the wise men (Matt. 2:12), and Paul (Acts 16:9). These were ones that knew their God, but there are also accounts of those who didn't know God receiving dreams. In Genesis 40:5-22 it says,

> *Then the butler and the baker of the king of Egypt, who were confined in the prison, had a dream, both of them, each man's dream in one night and each man's dream with its own interpretation. And Joseph came in to them in the morning and looked at them, and saw that they were sad. So he asked Pharaoh's officers who were with him in the custody of his lord's house, saying, "Why do you look so sad today?" And they said to him, We each have had a dream, and there is no interpreter of it." So Joseph said to them, "Do not interpretations belong to God? Tell them to me, please." Then the chief butler told his dream to Joseph, and said to him, "Behold, in my dream a vine was before me, and in the vine were three branches; it was as though it budded, its blossoms shot forth, and its clusters brought forth ripe grapes. Then Pharaoh's cup was in my hand; and I took the grapes and pressed them into Pharaoh's cup, and placed the cup in Pharaoh's hand." And Joseph said to him, "This is the interpretation of it: The three branches are three days. Now within three days Pharaoh will lift up your head*

and restore you to your place, and you will put Pharaoh's cup in his hand according to the former manner, when you were his butler. But remember me when it is well with you, and please show kindness to me; make mention of me to Pharaoh, and get me out of this house. For indeed I was stolen away from the land of the Hebrews; and also I have done nothing here that they should put me into the dungeon." When the chief baker saw that the interpretation was good, he said to Joseph, " I also was in my dream, and there were three white baskets on my head. In the uppermost basket were all kinds of baked goods for Pharaoh, and the birds ate them out of the basket on my head." So Joseph answered and said, "This is the interpretation of it; The three baskets are three days. Within three days Pharaoh will lift off your head from you and hang you on a tree; and the birds will eat your flesh from you." Now it came to pass on the third day, which was Pharaoh's birthday, that he made a feast for all his servants; and he lifted up the head of the chief butler and of the chief baker among his servants. Then he restored the chief butler to his butlership again, and he placed the cup in Pharaoh's hand. But he hanged the chief baker, as Joseph had interpreted to them.

Here are two men confined in prison who each have a dream: the butler and the baker. Neither knew the God of Abraham, Isaac, and Jacob, yet God had given them a dream. The interpretations and fate of each differed, one ending in death and the other in restoration to his position as butler. In this particular case, I believe that God wanted to establish Joseph's gift as an interpreter of dreams. Even though this may have been God's purpose, He indeed spoke to those who did not know Him. Another place in scripture where God spoke to an unrighteous individual is in Matthew 27:19:

> *While he was sitting on the judgment seat, his wife*
> *sent to him, saying, have nothing to do with that*
> *just Man, for I have suffered many things today in*
> *a dream because of Him.*

This scripture is referring to Pilot's wife. Jesus had been brought before Pilot for judgment and his wife received a distressing dream concerning Jesus so she delivered a warning to her husband. There are more scriptural accounts where God has brought a message in the way of a dream to one who was not in right standing with Him. God spoke through dreams to Pharaoh (Genesis 41:1-7), Abimelech (Genesis 20:3-7), and Nebuchadnezzar (Daniel 2:1). These are just a few accounts of dreams that came to the unrighteous. God is speaking, even now more than ever as the last days are approaching. Will we hear what He is saying? Now that the foundation has been laid and we see that God indeed speaks to us through dreams, it is time to look at the types of things that God may speak to us in our dreams.

Chapter 2

The Messages from God

When I finally realized that God was speaking to me in dreams, a new question arose. What in the world could God be saying to me? After all, most of my dreams didn't seem to make the least bit of sense but rather appeared to be a jumbled mess of my imagination gone wild!

Once again I realized that if I wanted to discern the types of messages that God might be speaking, I would need to go to the Bible for my answers. To my amazement, I found that God has much to say to us in our dreams. We will discuss at least eight of the different kinds of things that God may speak to us, but realize that God is not limited to these findings.

Words of Knowledge

A word of knowledge is a supernatural revelation by the Holy Spirit of a certain fact or facts. These facts can be about the past or the present. Often times, God will speak a word of knowledge in your dreams. This would be a piece of information that you could not have possibly known except by the Spirit of the Lord. Let's take a look at a dream from the scriptures that disclosed a word of knowledge.

> *But God came to Abimelech in a dream by night, and said to him, "Indeed you are a dead man*

> *because of the woman whom you have taken,* **for**
> **she is a man's wife.**" *But Abimelech had not*
> *come near her and he said, "Lord, will You slay a*
> *righteous nation also?* **Did he not say to me,**
> **"She is my sister, even she herself said, He is my**
> **brother.**" *In the integrity of my heart and*
> *innocence of my hands I have done this." And*
> *God said to him in a dream, "Yes, I know that you*
> *did this in the integrity of your heart. For I also*
> *withheld you from sinning against Me, therefore I*
> *did not let you touch her. Now therefore, restore*
> *the man's wife; for he is a prophet, and he will*
> *pray for you and you shall live. But if you do not*
> *restore her, know that you shall surely die, you*
> *and all who are yours" (Genesis 20:3-7).*

Preceding these verses we find that Abraham, our father of
faith, had journeyed to a new territory and was afraid that if
people knew that Sarah was his wife, he would be killed because
of her beauty. So Abraham decided to lie to protect himself.
Abimelech had no way of knowing that he had taken Abraham's
wife Sarah. Both Abraham and Sarah had told the king that they
were brother and sister. God gave Abimelech a word of
knowledge concerning his situation. God did this so that
Abimelech would not sin by committing adultery with Sarah. A
word of knowledge can be an important revelation when
discernment is needed, or it can also be a helpful tool in saving
someone's life just as it was for Abimelech. God said to him that
if he didn't restore her that he would die and all who were with
him.

I also have had a word of knowledge in a dream that has
saved a life. It saved the life of someone very close to me, my
mother. In this dream, my mother came to me with great concern
saying that there had been a problem with her mammogram so

the doctors wanted to reexamine her. I told my mother not to worry and that I would be there for her. I didn't take the dream seriously at first, basically forgetting about it until a few months later in my mother's living room while out-of-town relatives were visiting. The conversation turned to mammograms, which reminded me of my dream. So I asked my mother when she last had a mammogram. "Not for years," she answered. Immediately I felt prompted to impress upon her that she needed to be seen. She argued with me, using the excuse that she didn't like them (who does!). She emphatically insisted that she didn't have to tell me whether she got one or not, implying that I wouldn't know otherwise. I responded that she didn't have to tell me, but that God might. After a month or so of prodding her, she finally consented and went for her mammogram. Sure enough, there was a spot on it of some concern. The biopsy revealed that she indeed had cancer. When the doctor gave us the report, he said that fortunately this was the smallest amount of cancer that he had ever had to take out in his career. Praise God! He had given a word of knowledge that saved her life. Otherwise who knows if this would have ever been detected except in its late stages since my mom had such a negative attitude toward mammograms and wouldn't have had one without the constant prodding. Isn't God good? He knew it would take her a few months just to get the nerve to go for the test, and with this warning we were able to get the cancer at its beginning stages!

Warnings

God often will bring warnings through dreams. These warnings can be for yourself or someone else. I'm grateful when God warns me, whether it be to correct me or to prevent me from making a grave mistake. In the scripture about Abimelech's dream, we read about a word of knowledge, but also we can see that there is a word of warning that came in the form of a correction. God told Abimelech that if he didn't restore Abraham's wife, he was a dead man! I have had warning dreams that have been corrective and also those that prevent me from innocent error. Many times God has given me a warning dream for someone else to try to prevent them from making a mistake or even to spare one's life.

In the following scripture we will see that a warning was heeded, thus sparing the life of the child Jesus.

> *Then, being divinely warned in a dream that they should not return to Herod, they departed for their own country another way* (Matthew 2:12).

This scripture speaks of the wise men that had come to Jerusalem seeking the King of the Jews, the child Jesus. King Herod heard of this and called for the wise men to find out when the star appeared. He asked them to go and search carefully for the child, and when they found Him to bring back word that he too might come and worship the child. Of course, Herod had no intention of worshipping the child Jesus but planned to kill Him. God divinely warned these wise men concerning Herod so they returned a different way. Note that one man had the dream, but all heeded the warning. People more readily responded to dreams then than they do now. How many of us would respond to such a warning simply because someone said they had a warning dream? For our protection, God does give warnings in dreams and it is crucial to heed them.

As I said before, I am so grateful that God gives me warnings. I would certainly want someone to warn me if I were about to get hit by a Mack truck! Sometimes we have blind spots and need the help of another. I remember a warning dream I had for someone I hardly knew. It was not easy to reveal this serious dream to this person, but knowing the severity of the consequences, I chose to be bold by sharing the dream with this woman. I didn't know whether she would dismiss me as a fool, but her life was in danger — whatever she may have thought of me didn't matter in comparison to what she was about to experience.

In the dream I was riding in the back seat of a vehicle driven by this woman. She was driving on a straight-of-way, but her face was turned toward me to talk. Because we were on a straight road, it didn't seem to be dangerous until I noticed that the road was bending. I motioned to her by tilting my head to indicate that the road was bending, but she didn't understand. Finally, I made a dramatic move with my head and she took the bend with ease putting us back on a straight-of-way. However, she still kept her head turned towards me rather than the road. Suddenly a red jeep swerved into our lane — I knew we were doomed. I shut my eyes for the impact. When I opened them, I was in my same position unharmed (something that can happen only in dreams!) and the driver's door was open with her halfway onto the street. I rushed to help her, unsure whether she would live. I laid her on the ground, then noticed the jeep driver running towards the car as I awoke from my dream. I felt such despair in the dream out of concern as to whether she would live. Such a graphic dream like this with blood and all cannot be easily dismissed. It took two days for me to muster the courage to tell her the dream. She listened impassively till near the end. Incidentally, I did know that this woman's husband was in jail and was near his release time, but I didn't know his crime. When pondering the dream, I felt that the Lord gave me the interpretation that the man in the jeep was her husband who would cross the line. The woman would get the impact of that and might not make it through this. After telling her the dream, I quickly told her that I thought it pertained to her husband. Much to my surprise, she exclaimed that she agreed, saying that the telltale sign was the red jeep. That was her husband's favorite vehicle and the color he would choose if he were to buy one! God gave me that one little detail to confirm to her heart that God had a message for her. He loved her so much that He warned her of the impending danger. She told me that her husband had been physically abusive with her before and was in jail on domestic violence charges. He had been telling her how much he had changed and was trying to sweet-talk himself back into her home, but God protected her by giving her this word of warning through another individual's dream. God never ceases to amaze me. He is so awesome!

God has given me warnings about others concerning business transactions, prospective marriages and corrective type of warnings. He has warned me about people who are not on the "up-and-up" and spared me and others many mistakes. Sometimes these messages aren't the easiest to handle, but praise God that He will lead His people and keep their steps guarded!

Correction

From Abimelech's dream we see another word God may speak to us, and that is a word of correction. Often God will bring correction during our night seasons.

> *And God said to him in a dream, "Yes, I know that you did this in the integrity of your heart. For I also withheld you from sinning against Me; therefore I did not let you touch her. Now therefore restore the man's wife; for he is a prophet and he will pray for you and you shall live. But if you do not restore her, know that you shall surely die, you and all who are yours"* (Genesis 20:3-7).

God brought Abimelech a word of correction before he sinned against God by taking another man's wife. God commanded Abimelech to restore Abraham's wife back to him and to have Abraham pray for him so that he would live. Fortunately Abimelech heeded God's word and restored Sarah to Abraham. Because of his obedience, God opened the wombs of Abimelech's wife and his female servants so that they were able to bear children. Prior to this, God had closed all the wombs of the house of Abimelech because of Sarah. God will bring words of correction because it is His desire for us to walk in an overcoming and victorious life. Sometimes God will magnify things in dreams to get our attention because we ignore His correction when He speaks to us in other ways.

Prophetic Promises

One of the things I have found to be so awesome in my dreams is when God gives me a prophetic promise. There is nothing more exciting than a sneak preview of what God has ordained for you in the future. Seeing a glimpse of a promise helps you to remain faithful when you are enduring difficult times.

> *Now Joseph had a dream, and he told it to his brothers; and they hated him even more. So he said to them, please hear this dream which I have dreamed; there we were, binding sheaves in the field. Then behold, my sheaf arose and also stood upright; and indeed your sheaves stood all around and bowed down to my sheaf. And his brothers said to him, Shall you indeed reign over us? Or shall you indeed have dominion over us? So they*

> *hated him even more for his dreams and for his words. Then he dreamed still another dream and told it to his brothers, and said, Look I have dreamed another dream. And this time, the sun, the moon, and the eleven stars bowed down to me. So he told it to his father and his brothers; and his father rebuked him and said to him, What is this dream that you have dreamed? Shall your mother and I and your brothers indeed, come to bow down to the earth before you? And his brothers envied him, but his father kept the matter in mind.*
> (Genesis 37:5-12).

In this scripture, Joseph has been given prophetic promises concerning his future. God has shown Joseph what his future has to hold. He reveals that Joseph will be in a position of rulership. Indeed Joseph did become the governor of Egypt and his brothers did have to bow down before him. But between the dream and the fulfillment of his prophetic promise, Joseph endured many hardships such as being abandoned and sold into slavery by his brothers, and being accused of rape then left forgotten in prison for years. Joseph had his dreams to hold onto during the difficult times, and God brought Joseph favor with others even when he was facing challenging issues. In the end, Joseph attained all that God had promised him through those dreams.

In the same way that God spoke to Joseph concerning his future, God can speak to us. God may show you what your ministry or future career may be. Benny Hinn says, *"God often uses spiritual dreams and visions. In my own life, I would not be where I am today, if I had not taken my dreams seriously in my younger days."* I myself have had many prophetic promises. Some have already come to pass and some are in the process of fulfillment. God spoke to me years ago in a dream that I would be nationally acclaimed for dreams and the interpretation of dreams. I am beginning to see the fruit of this prophetic promise. I frequently get e-mail from people all across the country and in other nations such as South Africa and Singapore, asking for materials about dreams and the interpretation of dreams. It is amazing how these people have heard about my teaching and gifting concerning dreams and interpretations. God is faithful to do what He says He will do. There have been many other prophetic promises that I have had, and I hold dearly to those words as I await the promise. It helps to review those dreams when I am going through hard times. A dream can be like a video replaying in your mind when you feel you have no hope, and then that spark of hope returns after pondering the promise God has spoken in your dreams.

Direction

Probably my next favorite type of dream is that of direction. Many people feel it is wrong to look to dreams for direction. It can be a concern if you do not use wisdom and spiritually discern the timing of the direction being given. However, I have found that God gave much direction through dreams in both the Old and New Testaments, and I have found Him to direct me on many occasions through dreams.

> *And it happened, at the time when the flocks conceived, that I lifted my eyes and saw in a dream, and behold, the rams which leaped upon the flocks were streaked, speckled, and gray-spotted. Then the Angel of God spoke to me in a dream, saying Jacob. And I said, Here I am. And he said, Lift your eyes now and see, all the rams which leap on the flocks are streaked, speckled, and gray-spotted; for I have seen all that Laban is doing to you. I am the God of Bethel, where you*

anointed the pillar and where you made a vow to
**Me. Now arise, get out of this land, and return
to the land of your family** (Genesis 31:10-13).

In this passage of scripture God spoke to Jacob concerning his
living situation. God had seen that he had been mistreated for
years by his father-in-law Laban. God instructed Jacob to return
to the land of his family. Likewise, God may show you a
relocation change in your dreams.

> *And a vision appeared to Paul in the night. A*
> *man of Macedonia stood and pleaded with him,*
> *saying, "Come over to Macedonia and help us."*
> *After seeing the vision, immediately we sought to*
> *go to Macedonia concluding that the Lord had*
> *called us to preach the gospel to them* (Acts
> 16:9).

Here we read that Paul was prohibited by the Holy Spirit to enter
into Asia. I am sure that Paul had difficulty in understanding
why God would not allow him to go to Asia since he was told to
go into all the nations to preach the word of God. This dream
must have brought consolation to Paul when receiving it since
God directed him where he should go instead of Asia.

> *Now the birth of Jesus Christ was as follows:*
> *After His mother Mary was betrothed to Joseph,*
> *before they came together, she was found with*
> *child of the Holy Spirit. Then Joseph her*
> *husband, being a just man, and not wanting to*
> *make her a public example, was minded to put her*
> *away secretly. But while he thought about these*
> *things, behold, an angel of the Lord appeared to*
> *him in a dream, saying "Joseph, son of David, do*

> *not be afraid to take to you Mary your wife, for*
> *that which is conceived in her is of the Holy*
> *Spirit. And she will bring forth a Son and you*
> *shall call His name Jesus for He will save His*
> *people from their sins." So all this was done that*
> *it might be fulfilled which was spoken by the Lord*
> *through the prophet, saying: "Behold, the virgin*
> *shall be with child, and bear a Son, and they shall*
> *call His name Immanuel, which is translated, God*
> *with us." Then Joseph, being aroused from sleep,*
> *did as the angel of the Lord commanded him and*
> *took to him his wife, and did not know her till she*
> *had brought forth her firstborn Son. And he*
> *called His name Jesus* (Matthew 1:18-24).

Here again we see a directional word from the Lord. Joseph was definitely "stepping out in faith" to believe this dream. If dreams were not recognized as being a possible revelation from God, Joseph would have put Mary away to be stoned because she was pregnant with a child which did not belong to him. Thank God that Joseph had an understanding concerning dreams. God continued to direct Joseph in his dreams (See Matthew 2:13;19-22). Joseph didn't hesitate to obey the direction that God was giving him through his dreams.

When we think of receiving directional words in our dreams, we must consider a few matters. First, we must use caution as we learn to interpret our dreams. II Corinthians 13:1 says, "by the mouth of two or three witnesses every word shall be established." God will establish His word to you either through another witness or with other confirmations. It is good to get into the habit when you are lacking understanding to ask God for confirmation concerning your directional words. God is always happy to confirm His word to you if you lack understanding. We must also be careful to know the timing of a directional word.

Some words may be a "now" word, and others are for the future. Discerning the timing of words can be a challenge, but it will come through time and experience.

Future Revelation

God may choose to give you revelation that can pertain to a time far off. This revelation could happen during your lifetime or even beyond your lifetime. The revelation given to Daniel in the following verses pertained to an appointed time beyond his life span.

> *In the third year of Cyrus king of Persia a message was revealed to Daniel, whose name was called Belteshazzar. The appointed time was long; and he understood the message, and had understanding of the vision* (Daniel 10:1).

> *"Now I have come to make you understand what will happen to your people in the latter days, for the vision refers to many days yet to come"* (Daniel 10:14).

According to biblical time lines, this revelation did not come to pass for at least 500 years. Of course we can also see that John the Revelator received his vision of days to come and we are still awaiting the fulfillment and prophecy in the book of Revelations. We understand this future revelation to be around 2000 years old already!

Prophetic Word to People, Cities and Nations

One of the strangest words that I found to be given in a dream came from the book of Jeremiah. I was in my normal reading time when I stumbled upon a scripture that indicated that Jeremiah had received a prophetic word to the people of Israel through a dream. If you look at chapter 30 of Jeremiah and read from verse one all the way through chapter 31:25, you will find that Jeremiah was given a word from the Lord and in the verse directly following we read,

> *After this I awoke and looked around, and my sleep was sweet to me* (Jeremiah 31:26).

Under normal circumstances, I don't think I would have ever thought much of that scripture, but because God had been training me in the area of dreams and interpretations it became very evident to me. I have also experienced God giving me a message for a group of people through a dream. I was ready to go to Whitehorse, Canada, in the Yukon and just a few days prior to leaving for this ministry trip God gave me a dream with a prophetic word for the people of that area. It was a timely word and was confirmed by someone from that group of people who had received the same word just a year before. This was one of the easiest prophetic words I ever had to give!

Confirmation and Encouragement

God will often bring confirmation and encouragement in your dreams. When God began to heighten my discernment, He continually confirmed to me the things that He had told me. I kept tossing out revelation that God was giving me, thinking that it was my own thoughts, so God would give me dreams to confirm that it was Him all along. The following scripture is a great example of confirmation and encouragement.

> *When Silas and Timothy had come from Macedonia, **Paul was compelled by the Spirit**, and testified to the Jews that Jesus is the Christ. But **when they opposed him and blasphemed,** he shook his garments and said to them, "Your blood be upon your own heads; I am clean. **From now on I will go to the Gentiles.** " And he departed from there and entered the house of a certain man named Justus, one who worshipped God, whose house was next door to the synagogue. Then Crispus, the ruler of the synagogue, believed on the Lord with all his household. And many of the Corinthians hearing, believed and were baptized. Now the Lord spoke to Paul in the night by a vision, **"Do not be afraid, but speak, and do not keep silent; for I am with you, and no one will attack you to hurt you; for I have many people in this city"** (Acts 18:5-10).*

We see from this passage that Paul felt compelled by the Spirit to testify to the Jews, but when opposition came his way he felt like giving up and going to the Gentiles with the message of Christ. However, God spoke to Paul in a vision by night, confirming that he had been sent to these people and encouraging Paul to continue to work in that city. He told him not to be afraid or keep silent and that He was there for Paul. The scripture directly following these says that Paul continued on in that city for a year and six months. This dream gave Paul the confirmation and encouragement he needed to continue to do that which he had originally thought God had wanted him to do.

I appreciate the direct confirmation and encouragement that God will bring through my dreams. It is so easy to become discouraged when opposition arises as you do what the Lord has called you to do, but when words of encouragement come it helps to get your mind refocused and to keep you going in the direction He has sent you.

We have looked at many different types of messages that God may bring in our dreams. Perhaps if we understood why God desires to give us these types of messages, we might pay more attention to them. We will explore a few reasons in the following chapter.

Chapter 3

God's Purpose for Dreams

Why in the world would God want to speak to us in our night seasons? From the last chapter we saw that God will speak many types of words to us, but what is His purpose for this? I believe that God desires for us to have success in everything we do. In Proverbs 3:5,6 it says, "Trust in the Lord with all your heart, and lean not on your own understanding; In all your ways acknowledge Him and He shall direct your paths." We certainly cannot lean on our own understanding when it comes to the area of dreams. After all, they can seem to be quite bizarre at times. However, if we commit ourselves to God and allow Him to have access to any part of our lives, He will lead, guide, and direct us as a loving caring Father. Some of that leading may come in the form of a dream.

Instruction and Correction

Our loving Father desires us to prosper in all we do. Sometimes this requires much instruction and correction. In order to have a successful Christian walk we need to be directed by our nurturing Father.

*I will bless the Lord who has given me **counsel**;
My heart also **instructs** me in the night seasons.*
(Psalm 16:7)

*For God may speak in one way, or in another, yet
man does not perceive it. In a dream, in a vision
of the night, when deep sleep falls upon men,
while slumbering on their beds, then He opens the
ears of men and seals their **instruction. In order
to turn man from his deed,** and conceal pride
from man, **He keeps back his soul from the pit,**
and his life from perishing by the sword* (Job
33:14-18).

We can see from these scriptures that God desires to instruct
us in our night seasons. God wants to counsel us and bring
instruction to us. He does this whether we are awake or whether
we are asleep. I don't know about you, but I need all the
instruction and counsel I can get! I find that I don't always hear
God's instruction and counsel during my daytime hours because
of all of the responsibilities that I might have during a given day.
For this reason, I am so pleased that He speaks to me and I hear
Him during the night seasons. I heard one person say to me,
"Now that is what you call time management!" Indeed this is the
best time management you could ever attain, hearing God during
the day and then continually being instructed while you are
asleep. Only a great and awesome God could accomplish this!

Looking at the verses in Job, we see that God does this to turn
man from his wrong deeds in order to keep his soul from
perishing. When we look at the example we saw in the last
chapter concerning Abimelech, we see that God wanted to keep
this man's deed from causing him to sin against God which
would have resulted in Abimelech's perishing! God's instruction
saved this man from making a grave mistake!

Prayer

Another reason God may share dreams with you and give you words of knowledge is for prayer for the person or situation God is revealing to you. In John 15, Jesus tells us that no longer does He call us servants, but friends! He says this because a servant doesn't know what his master is about to do. In John 16, Jesus says that the Spirit of Truth will come and guide us into all truth and whatever He hears He will speak and He will tell us things to come. God will tell us things to come through our dreams. Some of what He tells us can be thwarted through prayer as is seen in the following scripture.

> *And the Lord said, "Shall I hide from Abraham what I am doing, since Abraham shall surely become a great and mighty nation, and all the nations of the earth shall be blessed in him? For* **I have known him**, *in order that he may command his children and his household after him, that they keep the way of the Lord, to do righteousness and justice, that the Lord may bring to Abraham what He has spoken to him." And the Lord said, "Because the outcry against Sodom and Gomorrah is great, and because their sin is very grave, I will go down now and see whether they have done altogether according to the outcry against it that has come to Me; and if not, I will know. Then the men turned away from there and went toward Sodom, but Abraham still stood before the Lord. And Abraham came near and said, "Would You also destroy the righteous*

*within the city; would You also destroy the place
and not spare it for the fifty righteous that were in
it? Far be it from You to do such a thing as this,
to slay the righteous with the wicked, so that the
righteous should be as the wicked; far be it from
You! Shall not the Judge of all the earth do
right?" So the Lord said, "If I find in Sodom fifty
righteous within the city, then I will spare all the
place for their sakes." Then Abraham answered
and said, "Indeed now, I who am but dust and
ashes have taken it upon myself to speak to the
Lord: Suppose there were five less than fifty
righteous; would You destroy all of the city for
lack of five?" So He said, "If I find there forty-
five, I will not destroy it." And he spoke to Him
yet again and said, "Suppose there should be
forty found there?" So He said, "I will not do it
for the sake of forty." Then he said, "Let not the
Lord be angry, and I will speak: Suppose thirty
should be found there?" So He said, "I will not
do it if I find thirty there." And he said, "Indeed
now, I have taken it upon myself to speak to the
Lord: Suppose twenty should be found there?"
So He said, "I will not destroy it for the sake of
twenty." Then he said, Let not the Lord be angry,
and I will speak but once more: Suppose ten
should be found there?" And He said, "I will not
destroy it for the sake of ten"* (Genesis 18:17-32).

God spoke to Abraham concerning the destiny of Sodom and
Gomorrah because he was God's friend! Abraham's immediate
response was to intercede on behalf of these two cities.
Abraham's prayer did not thwart God's plan for Sodom and
Gomorrah, but God did answer Abraham's prayer which was for

the righteous to be spared. Abraham's nephew Lot and his family were living in Sodom and Gomorrah. Abraham's faithfulness to pray kept Lot and his daughters from being killed along with the other inhabitants of these cities (Genesis 19). God may show you warning words of knowledge concerning a person or situation and prayer may be the key to keeping this calamity from coming to pass. In my life, I have seen prayer keep many destructive events from coming to pass. For example, one dream, I remember standing outside my home watching it go up in flames. I was grateful no one was trapped in the house, yet I felt despair and awkwardness witnessing all my life long possessions being destroyed before my eyes. (It is amazing how dreams can be so real and allow you to experience such emotions as I was feeling in this dream.) Boy, was I ever glad when I awoke to find it was just a dream! However, after contemplating the dream, fear began to race through my heart: What if this was a warning dream? Perhaps it had a spiritual meaning, but what if it was a reality of something that may happen? Even if this dream wasn't literal, I still felt that it did not have a good interpretation! Immediately I went to prayer: "Lord, I don't know if this dream is literal or not, but I ask You to preserve my home and protect it from any harm. Cover our home with Your blood and all our possessions. In Jesus name, amen." After praying, I was able to fall back to sleep. I wouldn't know until months later the effects of my prayers. It happened when our family was out of town except for my older son, then 19. Normally after work my son would visit his girlfriend, but this particular evening he came home after work. (This was very abnormal for him since he wanted to spend every waking hour with the love of his life!) Upon entering the house, he smelled smoke. He searched the house for the source but found nothing. Finally he narrowed the smell down to the livingroom. There he found my mug warmer had been knocked off the end table upside down and had burned a six-inch hole in the carpet clear to the floorboard. (Presumably our cat bumped the mug warmer which switched on when striking the floor.) Later the carpet repairman said the carpet is so flammable that our house should have gone up in flames! God is so good! I realized afresh that day how prayer can change things: Our house fire had been thwarted because of prayer! Later a friend added a fun little picture to my tale, commenting, "There must have been angels all around that mug warmer huffing and puffing as they were blowing out that fire, exclaiming, 'She prayed for this one! We have a job to complete. Her son is almost here, keep going!'" Whether or not there were angels working hard to stop my fire, God had intervened because of my prayer.

To Help Others

Often God may give you a dream not for your personal benefit, but for the benefit of another. I have had numerous dreams that made no sense to me, but as soon as I told it to the person in my dream, it helped them tremendously. Note this scriptural example of that same thing:

> *And when Gideon had come, there was a man telling a dream to his companion. He said, "I have had a dream; to my surprise, a loaf of barley bread tumbled into the camp of Midian; it came to a tent and struck it so that it fell and overturned, and the tent collapsed." Then his companion answered and said, "This is nothing else but the sword of Gideon the son of Joash, a man of Israel! Into his hand God has delivered Midian and the whole camp." And so it was, when Gideon heard the telling of the dream and its interpretation, that he worshiped. He returned to the camp of Israel, and said, "Arise, for the Lord*

has delivered the camp of Midian into your hand"
(Judges 7:13-15).

Here Gideon overheard another man's dream that gave Gideon the courage to go forth and gain victory in the battle against the Midianites. Gideon needed this encouraging word from God since God had reduced his army from 20,000 to 300 soldiers (Judges 7). How much greater impact it must have had on Gideon to hear the dream and the interpretation come from the opposing camp! Isn't God good?!

God may give you a dream for another person, or you may be the one who benefits from another person's dream. Although God has given me many dreams that have benefited others, I also have been the recipient of another person's dream that benefited me. This dream came from a neighbor who was not aware of my situation. When she came to me, she said that she had this dream a few days earlier but was unable to get it out of her mind and decided to share it with me in hopes of her not having to give it further thought. In her dream, she had given me a ride to a courthouse where I was going to see if I could help a little boy. As I went ahead into the courthouse, she parked the car. As she was coming from the car, she spotted my Bible left outside on the courthouse steps. My bible was smoldering and a woman at the top of the steps was hosing them down and spraying my Bible. My friend thought of how important and irreplaceable this Bible was to me since I would write side notes throughout it as the Lord would speak to me. She ran up the steps to go into the courthouse to find me. Upon entering the foyer, she saw me coming down some stairs crying. Upon asking me what was wrong, I told her it was too late because they had already killed the little boy. Then the dream ended. This alarming dream meant nothing to her, but I knew exactly what it meant. God was letting me know that I was about to go ahead of Him in a situation that would have ultimately killed all that the Lord had been working to establish. My leaving the Bible outside the steps of the courthouse represented this. Thank God for her dream because it spared me of a big mistake that would not only have hurt me but also would have hindered the work that God was doing in another person. What meant nothing to my friend was an important message for me.

God will instruct, correct, encourage, prophesy and also bring confirmation to us in order to help turn us back from doing wrong deeds and to direct our paths. I appreciate the fact that God does not leave us in the dark, but gives us instruction that brings light into the night seasons.

PART II:

WHERE DO YOUR DREAMS COME FROM?

Chapter 4

Divine or Divination

Imagine that you have just awakened from a dream that seemed so real. You are still feeling the emotional impact when you finally realize that you were only dreaming. What a relief! Yet you can't help but wonder how you could have had a dream with such reality and great magnitude.

As I said earlier, at first I considered my dreams merely to be part of my vivid imagination or caused by something that I had eaten the night before. In my hunger to know the truth concerning dreams, I stumbled upon information that just didn't bear witness with my spirit. Some of it would make sense, yet much of it would leave me with an uneasy feeling. I would suppose that there was truth in much of what I read, but there was also a lot of speculation and myth. Among these articles and books, I found New Age attitudes and scientific approaches to explain the phenomena of dreams. Scientists have verified that we dream, but rather than exploring their theories as to how dreams are produced, I chose to go to the manual that would give me the true answers. This was not a science or history book, per se. It was the manual inspired by the creator of dreams Himself, the Bible. It is through the findings of the Word of God and the instruction of the Holy Spirit that I now share the answers I received.

Can Satan Give Me Dreams?

A few weeks before I was to present one of my Dream Seminars, I received a phone call about a TV program, which in previous episodes had referred to some dreams. The caller suggested that I watch it. So I watched the show and indeed the first story during this episode involved a person's dream. In this particular story, a house was on fire with two boys trapped inside. One of the boys was sound asleep in an upstairs room. As the story reported, the boy had a dream in which his father came to him and told him to wake up and flee the house. The boy woke up and realized that his room was filled with smoke. At this moment he immediately jumped out of his second-story room and landed safely in the yard. Before he could even make sense of the situation, he found out that his younger brother was still trapped inside the house. The older boy rushed back into the house and rescued his brother, to safety, then collapsed from the ordeal.

My heart was moved by this story and I had an immediate interpretation to the dream. As the program gave an explanation of the dream, I became very grieved and even enraged by it. A so-called dream specialist who had written a book on dreams was being interviewed. She was asked how dreams might play a part in our lives. Before this question, it was pointed out the father had died when the boy was about 2 years old. The woman interpreted the dream by saying that the spirit of this boy's dead father had come into the room and awakened him. That's when I became grieved in my spirit and then enraged by what was said. My understanding of this dream was that the boy's father represented the Heavenly Father who awoke the child to save him. Yet this "dream specialist" gave credit to the boy's dead father when God the Heavenly Father should have received the glory. In my righteous indignation something arose within me and I cried out to the Lord, "God, I now know why you have called me to this ministry. You should have received the glory for this dream! People are being led astray! I will go and proclaim your truths for as long as I am able!"

At this milestone I realized how hungry people are for the things of the spirit realm. Millions upon millions worldwide had viewed this program and would be quick to believe the woman's false interpretation because they have no other explanation. People are aware that there are spiritual truths and have many questions concerning them, but many people are being led astray in trying to find their answers. I also realized that Christians, in general are hesitant concerning the dream realm. Many are afraid that deception might occur if they took their dreams seriously, so much so that they won't even explore the truths concerning them. As long as I am able, I will speak out concerning the area of dreams and interpretations, and share what the Word of God has to say and the revelation the Holy Spirit has given me.

The Lord had given me a dream early on as He was beginning to draw my attention to the area of dreams. Its message was that I was to throw out everything I had previously learned concerning the area of dreams and interpretations and instead allow the Holy Spirit of Truth to teach me. As the Holy Spirit guided me throughout His Word, I was surprised by some of my findings. One of the greatest surprises I found during my in-depth study of the scriptures was that nowhere does it say that Satan can directly give us dreams. However, what I have found is that he can influence us in our heart or soul area, which I will cover shortly. First though, I want to note scriptures that refer to false dreams.

False Dreams

There are scriptures that refer to false prophecies and dreams and those who prophesy these lies or dream these dreams, such as the following from the Amplified Version.

> *"Concerning the prophets: My heart, says Jeremiah, is broken within me, all my bones shake; I am like a drunken man, a man whom wine has overcome, because of the Lord and because of His holy words which He has pronounced against unfaithful leaders. For the land is full of adulterers, forsakers of God, Israel's true Husband. Because of the curse of God upon it, the land mourns, the pastures of the wilderness are dried up. They both false prophets and people rush into wickedness; and their course is evil, their might is not right. For both false prophet and priest are profane; even in My house I have found their wickedness, says the Lord"* (Jeremiah 23: 9-11).

> *"And I have seen the folly in the prophets of Samaria; They prophesy by Baal and caused My people Israel to err and go astray. I have seen also in the prophets of Jerusalem a horrible thing; they commit adultery and walk in lies; they encourage and strengthen the hands of evildoers, so that none returns from his wickedness. They have all of them become to Me like Sodom, and her inhabitants like Gomorrah"* (Jeremiah 23:13,14).

*Thus says the Lord of hosts; "Do not listen to the words of the false prophets who prophesy to you. They teach you vanity, emptiness, falsity, and futility and they fill you with vain hopes; **they speak a vision of their own minds** and not from the mouth of the Lord. They are continually saying to those who despise Me and the word of the Lord, the Lord has said; You shall have peace; and they say to everyone who walks after the stubbornness of his own mind and heart, No evil shall came upon you"* (Jeremiah 23:16,17).

"I did not send these false prophets, yet they ran; I did not speak to them, yet they prophesied. But if they had stood in My council, then they would have caused My people to hear My words, then they would have turned them, My people, from their evil way and from the evil of their doings" (Jeremiah 23:21,22).

*"I have heard what the prophets have said who prophesy lies in My name, saying, I have dreamed, I have dreamed visions on my bed at night. How long shall this state of things continue? How long yet shall it be in the minds of the prophets who prophesy falsehood, even the prophets of the **deceit of their own hearts**, who think that they can cause My people to forget My name by their dreams which every man tells to his neighbor, just as their fathers forgot My name because of Baal?"* (Jeremiah 23:25-27).

As we can see from these scriptures, God is declaring that He has not spoken these lies that the false prophets or dreamers are prophesying. He says that they are speaking these things out of the deceit of their own hearts or the vision of their own minds. You see, they wanted to walk after their own hearts and desires, so they would prophesy peace to the people when peace was not what God was saying. God says that they are strengthening the hands of evildoers so that none of them returns from his wickedness. When God says that they are causing His people to forget His name just as their fathers forgot His name because of Baal, He is talking about their going after the desires of their own hearts and not the desires of God. Baal here means "owner, master, lord or husband." It was considered a false god, a lifeless idol, generally represented by some form of nature. Israel had been following the idol of their own hearts and were in great sin during this time. The leaders and priests were walking in wickedness and deceit. Had they been prophesying by the mouth of God, they would have stopped their own sin and caused the rest of the people to turn from the evil of their ways. Their hearts were desiring to continue in their folly and sin, so they were proclaiming peace to the people as if to say that God was overlooking the sin and that blessing was coming to the land. This was a vision of their own minds, not from the mouth of God. Note that God said that the people spoke from their own hearts; He did not say that a spirit or the devil made them do it!

Now let's consider Ezekiel 13 (Amplified Bible).

> *And the word of the Lord came to me, saying, "Son of man, prophesy against the prophets of Israel who prophesy, and say to those who prophesy out of their own heart, 'Hear the word of the Lord!' Thus says the Lord God; "Woe to the foolish prophets, **who follow their own spirit and have seen nothing!**"* (Ezekiel 13:1-3).

They have envisioned futility and false divination, saying, "Thus says the Lord! But the Lord has not sent them; yet they hope that the word may be confirmed. Have you not seen a futile vision and have you not spoken false divination? You say, "The Lord says, but I have not spoken." Therefore thus says the Lord God: "Because you have spoken nonsense and envisioned lies, therefore I am indeed against you," says the Lord God (Ezekiel 13:6-9).

*"The prophets of Israel who prophesy concerning Jerusalem, and who see visions of peace for her when there is no peace," says the Lord God. Likewise, son of man, set your face against the daughters of your people, **who prophesy out of their own heart**; prophesy against them"* (Ezekiel 13:16,17).

Once again in these scriptures we see that they are prophesying out of their own hearts; they follow their own spirit and have seen nothing! In verses 6-9, it says that they have envisioned futility and false divination. Divination here means "lot, oracle, witchcraft." Its root word is "divine." Divination is a false oracle, claiming the word came from God. They were proclaiming the words they spoke to be a divinely inspired word, yet God did not give those words, which in turn misrepresented Him and is called divination. God says these words were inspired by their own hearts. Again we do not see that Satan had given these dreams. The devil did not make them do it! He may have influenced their heart realm through sin, but he did not directly give them their dreams. Let's take a closer look at how Satan might influence our dreams.

Heart and Soul

So how is it that our heart can play a part in our dreams? God said that the priests and prophets were speaking corruptly by the evil intents of their hearts or minds. I am going to explore this area of what He calls the heart, or what we might call the soul. I will intermix the words "soul" and "heart" because of how they relate so closely in the Hebrew. First, the meaning of heart in these verses means "your mind, your will, your emotions and your feelings." The meaning for soul is "a life, a living being, a self, a person, mind, personalities, inner desires and feelings." So as you can see, whether we refer to it as soul or heart we are talking about your mind, will, and emotions or inner desires and feelings. This is that inner part of you that makes the mind think, the will act and the emotions come forth. For the purpose of this teaching, I will refer back and forth from soul to heart. Our soul realm is the area where Satan can get his influence.

Let's see what the scriptures say concerning the heart or soul.

> *A good man out of the good treasure of his heart brings forth good; and an evil man out of the evil treasure of his heart brings forth evil. For out of the abundance of the heart his mouth speaks* (Luke 6:45).

Jesus teaches here that the heart will play a part in what comes out of our mouth, either good or evil. Before anything comes out of our mouth, it must first go through our mind. So we could reword part of this verse to say, "For out of the abundance of the heart, his mind dreams." What is in the heart is what is going to come forth. So out of the treasures of a good heart will come forth good dreams, and out of the treasures of an evil heart will come evil dreams. If heart means the mind, will and emotions, then it could be said, out of the good of our mind comes forth good and out of the evil of our mind comes forth evil. Or, out of the will would come forth either good or evil and out of our emotions would be either good or evil. Whatever is the content of our heart is going to come out, and it will come out in our dreams as well. Let's focus separately on the mind, the will and the emotions. We will determine in each area whether our dreams will be of a divine nature, or more carnal or fleshly which may appear demonic.

Mind

Colossians 3:2 says "to set your minds on things above, not on things of this earth." This means that we are to set our minds on things of the Spirit, not on the things we experience here on earth.

> *For those who live according to the flesh set their mind on the things of the flesh, but those who live according to the Spirit, the things of the Spirit. For to be carnally minded is death, but to be spiritually minded is life and peace* (Romans 8:5,6).

Those who will live according to the Spirit will receive life and peace. But if we set our minds on those things of our carnal nature, then we'll live by them, and to be carnally minded is death. Just what does it mean to be carnally minded? To be carnal in any way is to go after what our flesh desires. Galatians speaks about the fruit of the Spirit versus the works of the flesh.

> *Now the works of the flesh are evident, which are: adultery, fornication, uncleanness, lewdness, idolatry, sorcery, hatred, contentions, jealousies, outbursts of wrath, selfish ambitions, dissensions,*

heresies, envy, murders, drunkenness, revelries, and the like; of which I tell you beforehand just as I also told you in time past, that those who practice such things will not inherit the kingdom of God (Galatians 5:19-21).

There are many things that are spoken of in this scripture that relate to our carnal, fleshly nature. Most of us may not even think of being involved in some of these works of the flesh, such as murder or adultery; however, there are many things that we might allow our minds to absorb as we watch TV and movies, or read magazines and books that deal with these sins. If we are watching soap operas (which probably deal with every one of the works of the flesh listed in Galatians), then we are allowing our hearts or souls to be filled with carnal things. If we are putting things into our minds such as pornography, romance novels, movies or books of an evil nature, and even certain music, then we are filling our hearts with fleshly things. If we are filling our minds with such carnality, then what do you suppose is going to come out? Jesus said that out of the abundance of our hearts, our mouth speaks; or in this case, our mind dreams. This does not mean that you can't have divinely inspired dreams, but it will certainly make it more difficult to determine whether your dream is from God or your own soul realm. The more fleshly or carnal things that we put into us, the more likely we are going to be producing soulish dreams in our night seasons, dreams that are coming from our heart. But if you begin to put the things of the Spirit into your heart, such as the Word of God, anointed teaching tapes or videos, Christian music and books, the more likely you will be to weed out a lot of the soulish dreams and begin to recognize more of the divinely inspired dreams. This does not mean that you won't experience soulish dreams, but you will find that you recognize the divinely inspired dreams more readily. (There are other factors we will explore which may cause a person to dream soulish dreams.) We want to be able to determine which of our dreams are from God and which are from our own hearts.

> *Finally brethren, whatever things are true, whatever things are noble, whatever things are just, whatever things are pure, whatever things are lovely, whatever things are of good report, if there is any virtue and if there is anything praiseworthy, meditate on these things* (Philippians 4:8).

God exhorts us to get ourselves free of the carnal debris and to keep our minds healthy by thinking of those things which are good. Remember the Sunday school song: "Be careful little eyes what you see, be careful little ears what you hear," and so forth. There is an important message in those lyrics. We teach our children to be careful about what they allow into their little spirits, yet we adults think we can go unaffected by what we allow our eyes to see and ears to hear. Not true! We are damaging our hearts or souls just as much as our children would.

Will

Our will is the area where we make choices. We make the choice whether to obey or disobey God. What happens when we choose to disobey God? We produce sin in our life. Sin can really damage our soul area. We need to be healed from the sins of our past.

> *I said, "Lord, be merciful to me; Heal my soul, for I have sinned against You"* (Psalm 41:4).

Basically what David is saying in this scripture is, "Lord be merciful to me, My soul is in need of healing because of my sin against You." David knew that sin and disobedience to God would scar his soul. He needed to be healed from that. He had sinned against God through adultery with Bathsheba and by murdering her husband to cover up his sin. These sins marred David's soul. We have sins of our past, some "before Christ" and some "after Christ," which have marred and affected our soul. These areas have need of healing. Through our sin we have brought damage to our soul. Because of these sins and the damage and affect they have on our hearts, we may find that these unhealed wounds will erupt in our dreams. Perhaps some behaviors of your past that you thought were put away, start showing up in your night seasons. I know that I have had things come in my dreams that I have to say have not been part of my life or thought patterns in a long time. It's hard for me to even imagine that some of these things are in my heart since I seemed to be so far removed from them; but in actuality, these are sins of my past that are still in need of healing. Just as David cried out, "Heal my soul, for I have sinned against You," I am saying, "God heal my soul of these sins!" As we progress in this teaching we will see what we can do about these types of soulish dreams. For now, let's see how our emotions affect our dream life.

Emotions

Emotions are affected by our past hurts. Any emotion that is not a godly emotion is not a good emotion. When God created us, He created us with perfect souls. We had been protected in our mother's womb from the sin and defilement that would later come because of this sin-filled world we were about to enter. Also, because we have a sin nature, sin appeared very early in our lives without much effort on our parts to exercise it. When sin enters in, then come hurts from which we need healing, and that in turn will affect our emotions. Anger, rage, and jealousy are ungodly emotions. These kinds of emotions happen because of sin and wounds from our past. Some of the emotions we experience and develop can be caused by the defilement that was done at the hands of other people.

> *Our soul is exceedingly filled with the scorn of those who are at ease, with the contempt of the proud* (Psalm 123:4).

Many of us may have been born into difficult circumstances and situations. We didn't ask to be born in the environment that we were, but because of certain situations we become marred and our souls scarred by the effects of those environments. Some of you may have grown up with alcoholic parents, or perhaps you were brought up in an environment where drug dealers and prostitutes were the norm. Others may have been molested or physically abused throughout their childhood. These types of situations caused by others have filled our souls with various wounds and emotions that are unhealthy. Many times anger and rage is typically found among people who have been hurt by the ones who should have been nurturing them. We have need for God to heal and deliver us in these areas so that our emotions will line up with the way God created them to be. God gave us emotions. He expects that we will respond to different situations with different emotions. However, they need to be the godly emotions that we experience and not those emotions that come from an unhealed wound. Jesus experienced many emotions during His time on earth. He experienced joy, compassion, sorrow, grief and even anger, but without sin. When Jesus became angry and drove out all those who bought and sold in the temple and overturned the tables of the money-changers, His anger was not because of a past wound or hurt. His anger was a righteous anger concerning the way the house of God was being used. The scripture challenges us, saying "Be angry, but do not sin and do not let the sun go down on your wrath" (Ephesians 4:26). We are to hate sin and its effects but we are not to hate the sinner. Our anger should only be concerning the sin and should not be carried over on a daily basis. When we have emotions with fits of jealousy, anger and rage driven by past wounds or hurts, we have need of healing and deliverance, because this type of emotion produces sin. Often times, we don't know the conditions of our hearts and may think that we are doing just fine, but things can be so hidden within us that we aren't even aware there is a problem.

> *Both the inward thought and heart of man*
> *are deep* (Psalm 64:6b).

Sometimes when God wants to bring the awareness and healing of a wound to us, we will begin to have dreams and start to see these behaviors and emotions in them. Because the thought and inward heart of man is deep, it takes some digging by the Holy Spirit to expose them. When they are exposed, generally the emotions will gush forth in a magnified manner.

I experienced this in my own life. By way of background, I grew up in a fatherless home. My mother did her best to raise us, but things happened to me that were beyond her control. I was molested at a very early age which made me an angry child who rebelled as a teenager. My rebellious behavior scarred my soul. These sins, along with the scorn from others, left wounds hidden deep in my heart. Because of these wounds and a desire to be loved and accepted, I became sexually active and found myself pregnant right after graduating from high school. I married the father of this child, a man who abused me on a daily basis for the four years of our marriage. (I didn't realize I was abused because it didn't come in the form of a fist, but found out later that verbal abuse can be more damaging than any physical bruise or broken bone.) Needless to say, many more wounds were added to my soul. I later became a Christian and God gave me a wonderful godly husband.

A few years into my current marriage, my husband said to me, "Well, that was really stupid." He meant it in a lighthearted manner, but when I heard the word "stupid," I exploded. Words and reactions that I hadn't used or expressed in years came gushing forth. My rage was unparalleled and all consuming. I couldn't believe my reaction, a reformed Christian woman who loved her life and husband, but you wouldn't have known it by looking at my behavior. My husband stared at me in astonishment, probably asking himself, "Who is this raging woman?!" I don't remember how long I was a maniac, but angry words seemed to keep rolling out of the depths of my inner being. When it finally subsided, I had to look at myself in the mirror and ask, "Who was this person?" All along I was not aware that I needed to be healed of the verbal abuse I had endured during my first marriage. I had taken my husband's comment personally as though he were calling me "stupid" because of the hurt that still resided within. I was unaware of my need for healing because it had been hidden in the deep recesses of my heart. God was gracious to me by allowing this wound to be exposed so that I could be healed and delivered of the hurt that was still inside.

My husband does not remember this incident for which I am grateful, but I will never forget how God showed me that we are unaware of all the scorn and pain within our hearts. God came to set us free and to give us eternal life not just for the hereafter, but also for the here and now. We can walk in complete healing right here on earth! God wants us healed and He will use dreams to bring that healing. I have seen the same kind of behavior that I just shared with you show up in my dreams over other unhealed wounds. I am thankful that God will now use dreams to show me where I have need of healing; that way, I don't have to fly off the handle at someone else's expense!

Another way our emotions can affect our dreams is through our desires. Sometimes being deprived of something as we grew up will cause us to have an unhealthy desire as adults. If we lacked love, we may see that desire for love overcome by lust. If we lacked financial blessing, we may be overcome by greed. Some of our desires have been given by God, but many come from an emotional need to find the fulfillment and peace that can only come through an intimate relationship with Jesus. Our true fulfillment comes only from God. As we receive emotional healing, we will recognize which desires have been deposited by God and which originated from our lack.

A woman once told me that she had many dreams about becoming pregnant and having a baby. She was certain and determined that God was going to give her a baby even though her husband had a vasectomy. This woman was already blessed with one healthy child, although she had experienced a few miscarriages. She felt deprived since she had not had more children. Because of her desire for more children and the wounds that still remained from the miscarriages, she would often dream of having a baby. She believed the dreams were telling her that she would become pregnant, just as she desired. God wanted to bring healing to her concerning her losses, but she mistakenly thought that she would have a literal pregnancy. Our emotions can mislead us when it comes to our dreams. It is so important that we receive inner healing so we are able to discern whether our dreams are divinely inspired rather than soul dreams which can be inspired by the deceit of our own hearts.

What Do We Do Now?

We have seen that what is in our heart or soul can indeed influence our dreams. For out of the abundance of our heart (mind, will, and emotions) our mouths will speak or shall we say, our minds will dream. So what can we do about the abundance of what is in our hearts, or these soul dreams?

> *I beseech you therefore brethren, by the mercies of God, that you present your bodies a living sacrifice, holy, acceptable to God, which is your reasonable service.* ***And do not be conformed to this world, but be transformed by the renewing of your mind,*** *that you may prove what is that good, acceptable and perfect will of God* (Romans 12:1,2).

This scripture exhorts us to change our thinking and actions. We are not to be like the world, but we are to be transformed into the image of Christ Jesus. We can only renew our minds if we fill them with the Word of God! It is His Word that can bring the healing we desire and transform us to become like Jesus.

> *For the word of God is living and powerful and sharper than any two-edged sword, piercing even to the division of soul and spirit, and of joints and marrow, and is a discerner of the thoughts and intents of the heart* (Hebrews 4:12).

The Word of God is powerful enough to discern the thoughts and intents of our hearts. As we fill ourselves with the Word of God and let it consume us, our soul will be transformed.

> *The law of the Lord is perfect, converting the soul* (Psalm 19:7a).

God's word is perfect and it will convert our souls! The word "convert" here in the Hebrew means to "take back and restore it to its original state." Glory to God! He can heal the soul and bring it back to the original state He created it to be, long before all the scorn and sin marred our soul. But we can see that we have a responsibility to do something. We are responsible to correct the negative behavior in our lives.

> *If then you were raised with Christ, seek those things which are above, where Christ is, sitting at the right hand of God. Set your minds on things above, not on things on the earth. For you died, and your life is hidden with Christ in God* (Colossians 3:1-3).

We are to seek heavenly things and set our minds on the things above, not what is here on earth. We also need to remove the fleshly appetites and pet sins we carry.

> *Therefore put to death your members which are on the earth; fornication, uncleanness, passion, evil desire, and covetousness, which is idolatry* (Colossians 3:5).

Yes, and not only are we to put off our fleshly appetites but also those things we may not consider to be sin!

> *But now you yourselves are to put off all these; anger, wrath, malice, blasphemy, filthy language out of your mouth* (Colossians 3:8).

By taking an active part in obedience to these words of God, we will begin to see that our soul dreams will become less frequent and as a result we should be able to recognize the divinely inspired dreams more readily! So what else can we do about these soul dreams?

Second, we need to begin to recognize the areas in which we need healing. We can begin to recognize those areas by examining our dreams. I don't toss out any dream even if I have concluded that it came from my soul. I find that God can use these soul dreams to speak into my heart if I will let Him. I use my soul dreams as a barometer to gauge where my heart is and whether there are issues or sins that I need to deal with. God will reveal to me, through my soul dreams, where I may need to apply forgiveness to someone or an incident that I may never have let go of. I remember one dream that showed I still held unforgiveness towards someone who for many years I professed to have forgiven. What a shock for me to find out I never really had forgiven this person. Upon analyzing this soul dream, I was able to determine that I had never really let go of the pain that I felt was suffered at the hands of this person. At the point of awareness, I was able to confess my own unforgiveness towards this individual and then forgive the person. What a good feeling when you truly release a person of their sin against you! Praise God for the soul dream that revealed the condition of my heart! I still get soul dreams and sometimes it can be hard to take a closer look at them. Just about the time I think I am moving onto maturity and perfection, a soul dream will occur which sets me right back into the humble place I belong. But I am thankful for these dreams because the Word says that "pride cometh before the fall," and if I think that somehow I have attained near perfection, then I need to see the actual condition of my soul. That in itself should keep me humble!

What is the condition of your heart? Are your dreams giving you an indication? By applying the truths in this chapter, you can move on to growth and maturity in God through the evaluation of your dreams. God is speaking and we want to hear what He is saying to us. Hopefully you have a new understanding of how you can discern between a divinely inspired dream and one that comes from the soul, and how you can use your soul dreams as a barometer to review the condition of your heart.

Chapter 5

R-Rated Dreams

What if you have known and applied the truths spoken about in the preceding chapter, yet still find yourself having dreams that appear to be demonic or extremely carnal. One thing I don't want you to do is label all seemingly carnal dreams or those that appear demonic as soulish. Just because you have a dream that appears to be R-rated does not guarantee that it could not have come from God. There are times when you will find God speaking a message to you through such dreams.

Dreams with Sexual Content

I can remember the first dream I had which seemed totally out of character for me. This dream came even after I had been applying the truths from chapter four and had already received much healing on major issues. I woke from this dream and wondered just what it could have meant. This dream began with me walking home after being seen by a doctor who had told me that I was pregnant. I was pondering how I was going to tell my husband this information, especially since I knew that the baby was not his. In my mind I didn't know how this had happened. I knew that even if I had wanted to, I could not pass this child off as my husband's because this child's father was from a different nationality. How could I tell my husband this news? What would he do? Upon entering the house, I told him that I had some news and he replied that he already knew. I was shocked that he had known, but exclaimed that I didn't know how it happened — I never did anything! I was defending myself because I didn't know how this happened. But my husband had a comeback to my every word. He believed the report of the pregnancy and couldn't believe in my innocence. When I awoke my pounding heart was nearly in my throat. I wondered what this dream was all about. My immediate thoughts were that I must have misunderstood somehow the things that God had taught me about dreams and reckoned within myself that Satan had given me this dream. I knew that I had never done anything like this dream suggested, and believe that I never would. Once I chalked this dream up to Satan, I thought it would go away, but it wouldn't leave me. God finally gave the interpretation of this dream to me, but only after I had suffered for what seemed like an eternity, yet had only been a few hours! God said to me, "You are indeed pregnant and this child is not of the same race because you are pregnant with ministry that the Holy Spirit has given you and you will not be able to pass this off as being your husband's because this is Mine!" Wow! How tremendous! And to think that I had blamed the whole dream on Satan! Now any person would have thought this dream to have been from the enemy or at least our old carnal nature. But the dream was from God! Not everything that appears to be carnal is from our soul. I have awakened many times sweating and concerned over what I had just seen or experienced in a dream. (With such dreams, I am always glad to find out that I was only dreaming!)

God is not a prude and He may give you some dreams that will have you sure they couldn't be from Him, yet they are. Of course, many of these will not be divine, especially if we continue to walk in the things of this world and satisfy our fleshly desires. Yet God has recorded some risqué things in the scripture which confirms that He is not a prude. In the book of

Ezekiel, God refers to Jerusalem, His people, as harlots! In Hosea, God tells the prophet Hosea to marry a prostitute as a prophetic drama of His unconditional love for His people. God told Isaiah to run around naked for three years prophesying to everything in sight! He told Ezekiel to lie on his side for a year and cook his food over human waste! Ezekiel argued with God that he had never defiled himself with anything and he wasn't about to do it now, so God allowed him to use cow dung instead (some improvement)! Such examples show that God isn't concerned about offending us or sparing our "holy ears" from hearing such things. God wants to speak to us and sometimes He will get downright blunt! He is going to speak in a language that we will understand.

Sometimes those earthly dreams can be quite troubling. The first thing we need to do with an R-rated dream is rule out the soul area. What has been the condition of our soul? Have we been putting in garbage? (Garbage in, garbage out!) Once we have examined our soul, we need to ask God to reveal the interpretation. Perhaps God is wanting to encourage us (such as my dream I mentioned above), or maybe He is revealing how He sees the condition of the Church. God described His people as harlots; He may show us how He sees things that we don't consider offensive, just to get His point across.

Dreams of a Demonic Nature

Some dreams appear to be demonic because they may include snakes, demonic-looking beings and the like. Such dreams would appear to have Satan's fingerprints all over them. Well, as discussed above, what we put into our minds will sooner or later begin to come out. So if we are watching horror films or reading horror stories, then it will be likely for us to see this kind of stuff in our night seasons. Or if someone has been involved in cult activities, they may have a dream of this nature. However, if you haven't done these things and there is no known reason for such content in your dreams, then it is likely that these dreams are from God.

When I first began to experience these types of dreams, I had so much paralyzing fear that I could not even muster the words, "In the Name of Jesus!" Some would argue that God wouldn't give those kinds of dreams, but I would beg to differ on that point. God will use things of a demonic nature to speak some things to you. He may speak a warning to you, or show you the enemy's plot or attack on another person. He may just want to bring you into the knowledge, that "greater is He that is in us than he that is in this world." I know this is one thing He did with me. In one dream I saw a spirit hovering over me and, feeling paralyzed by it, was hardly able to speak the name of Jesus. Only after much effort was I able to get the name "Jesus" to escape from my vocal cords. Upon waking, I felt defeated realizing that as a child of the living God I should not be at fear and should have no problem using the name of Jesus to help me. God brought this revelation to me and then continued to give me similar dreams. In each dream, I grew stronger and bolder in my spirit. It became easier to declare the name of Jesus, and every time I did the spirit would have to flee! Once I was so angry with the enemy that I spoke matter-of-factly ordering him to leave because of the authority which had been given me by Jesus! Wow! I no longer feared the enemy or what he might think he could do to me. God helped me to come to that realization through these seemingly demonic dreams. I am not saying it wasn't difficult to have those dreams and there are times when the hair on the back of my neck can stand up, but I now know the authority I have been given through the name and blood of Jesus.

Once a friend who was soon to minister in Mexico told me about some dreams she had just before her trip which she felt were from Satan. In the dreams, witch doctors were putting curses on her. I told her not to be so sure the dream wasn't from God, that He might be showing her impending spiritual attack in order for her to deal with it in the Spirit before her departure. The Word promises, "No weapon formed against you shall prosper and every tongue that rises up against you shall be condemned." God was allowing her to know the enemy's plan of attack so that she wouldn't enter Mexico unaware of the spiritual warfare she was about to encounter. Praise God for such warning dreams!

God used very graphic imagery when speaking to Daniel. So much so that Daniel says he was grieved in his body for days by what he saw.

> *And I, Daniel, fainted and was sick for days; afterward I arose and went about the king's business. I was astonished by the vision, but no one understood it* (Daniel 8:27).

In the book of Revelation, most of what John envisioned appeared to be of a demonic nature. He saw snakes, dragons, four-headed creatures and other wild things. These visions and dreams were from God, yet they appeared to be purely demonic. We would have to toss out half the book of Revelation if we thought that God wouldn't give these types of dreams.

If you are being prepared for a deliverance ministry, God may use dreams to teach you about deliverance and the authority and power you have in Him to overcome the enemy. He may show you some frightening stuff, otherwise how would you be prepared to meet a person like the one described in Luke 8:26-39? This demoniac was probably the worst of any that Jesus delivered. He had a legion of demons and must have been a grotesque sight; however, one cannot fear a demon-possessed person if they are going to have a deliverance ministry. Sometimes when Jesus cast out a demon, the demon would seize the person and cast them to the ground where they would convulse and then lay as dead, only later to discover they were delivered! Suppose you are called to a third-world country that openly serves false gods and has major witchcraft activity, or called to those who have been involved with the occult, even performing satanic rituals. There you will encounter people who need major deliverance, but if you cannot handle seeing the effects these spirits have on people in your dreams, then you will not be able to handle them in reality. I have seen some grotesque things in my dreams because God has wanted me prepared to set the captives free. Sometimes in setting people free, you will see manifestations of demons, and if you haven't been prepared, you will most likely not know how to walk in your authority when the need arises.

Children and Nightmares

What about dreams or nightmares that your children have? I have very prophetic children who often have spiritual dreams. Sometimes these dreams will frighten them. I have been able to understand some of their dreams and they have brought encouragement, direction and warning. It is amazing that even dreams that appear to be bad can be helpful. Our eight-year old daughter recently dreamed about two snakes chasing me up our stairway. She said that Sue Ellen stomped on the heads of the snakes, killing them before they were able to bite me. This dream came at a very crucial time because I was experiencing opposition without fully realizing that it was a spiritual attack. There are times when an attack can come and you think it is merely "works of the flesh." God brought the message to me through my daughter's dream, though, that I was actually dealing with spiritual assault.

There have been times when I have not understood at all some of the dreams my children have had which appeared to have been nightmares. I strongly desired to understand why some of these dreams were occurring because of what I felt that God had shown me scripturally that Satan cannot directly give us dreams. I have always tried to be very cautious about what I allow my children to watch on TV or movies and also what books they read, so I was unable to understand why my son was having bad dreams. I went before the Lord hoping for an answer. God finally showed me through a dream why my child was having bad dreams. In this dream, my son came to me saying that he had a bad dream. I asked, "What have you been watching on TV?" He answered, "Dungeons and Dragons." I don't believe that son was ever watching anything on TV with that title, and I am sure that he was not involved in the Dungeons and Dragons game. But there are many TV cartoons with dragons and other seemingly "cute" creatures. These cartoons subtly penetrate our children's souls without our awareness. Even though many of the cartoons have these cute little non-threatening characters, they contain much violence and magic, along with spiritual forces of other dimensions. All this filters into our children's souls. Not only are many TV cartoons a threat, but so are many arcade and Nintendo games. These can be full of violence and demonic overtones while using cute little characters.

One of the worst of these is Pokemon. God exposed this cartoon to me very early so I would be aware and keep my children from watching the daily afternoon program. Not only does Pokemon have a cartoon, but also a movie, Nintendo game, collector cards and a board game. Pokemon is endangering our children with demonic influence while most Christian parents are unaware of the effects it can have on their children. A good book on this topic is *Buying and Selling the Souls of our Children* by John Paul Jackson. John Paul examines closely Pokemon and exposes its deception.

What God showed me about my son's nightmares was the necessity to be just as careful about what our children watch, even if the material seems juvenile. Parents, please take the time to examine what programs your children are viewing!

Now that we have seen that God can give dreams which appear demonic, let's explore another reason we may receive such dreams.

Chapter 6

Watchman Dreams

As we have learned, God can give many warning dreams. When warning dreams come often, it is usually a sign that God has made you a watchman. Watchman as defined in Strong's concordance means "to look out, peer into the distance, spy, deep watch, to scope something out, especially in order to see approaching danger, and to warn those who are in danger." It is translated "a king's guard, those who look out from a tower in the city wall." It can also be "a sentry, a guard, a soldier stationed to prevent unauthorized passage." The spiritual meaning is watchman or prophets who look out, see danger and report to the people.

> *"Son of man, I have made you a watchman for the house of Israel; therefore hear a word from My mouth, and give them warning from Me"* (Ezekiel 3:17).

A watchman does not have to be set over a city or country in order to be called a watchman, but can be set over a family, church or even a neighborhood. God has made me a watchman to my family and to many of my friends as well as over churches. It seems wherever I go to minister, the Lord will give me dreams which allow me to see the holes in the walls, or danger of attacks. He does the same in respect to my own children. God will show me the attempts of the enemy's attacks long before they begin to happen. This is what we would call peering out into the distance, spying the land. Dreams like these don't always make sense to our natural minds. Many times I will report a watchman dream to someone and they don't think that it applies to them because they can't see in the natural what God has shown in the spiritual.

When Joshua and the children of Israel entered the Promised Land, they discovered cities surrounded with strongly fortified protective stone walls. These walls were often very high and extremely wide.

> *"Where can we go up? Our brethren have discouraged our hearts, saying, "The people are greater and taller than we; the cities are great and **fortified up to heaven**; moreover we have seen the sons of the Anakim there"* (Dueteronomy 1:28).

The children of Israel exclaimed that these protective walls were up to the heavens. Their height made it easier for the guards upon the wall to see far. If you were to stand at the base of the wall and peer out, you wouldn't see very far into the distance, but the higher you are the farther you see. Thus, watchman were able to see potential danger approaching long before it reached the city. If they saw something suspicious, they needed to warn the king so the city could be prepared for an attack. This is why a watchman is so necessary. When I bring a warning dream to an individual or church, they have to trust that what I am saying is true because they cannot see in the natural or from the base of the wall what I am talking about.

> *For thus has the Lord said to me; "Go, set a watchman, let him declare what he sees"* (Isaiah 21:6).

Recently God gave me a parable of the importance of the watchman. At the time of this parable, I did not have an anti-virus protection program on my computer. Consequently, a virus infected the computer. Unaware of this, an attachment which spread the virus was sent to the people in my address book and spread the virus. Many of the recipients had a virus protection program and fortunately were warned concerning it. If my computer had this program, it would have alerted me to this problem and could have spared me the results of infected files. I learned a valuable lesson through this process.

We should all desire to have a watchman in our lives. They are able to see the blind spots that we are unable to see. Many problems could be avoided if, like the virus protection program, we were alerted to the potential danger the enemy has sent our way.

Because of the confidential information the Lord will disclose to a watchman, it is necessary for the watchman to receive training in this area. There is a maturing process one needs to undergo in order to be an effective watchman. (Rather than going into further detail here concerning the watchman, I will discuss the role and training of a watchman in my upcoming book, *Watchman, Watchman, What of the Night.* This book will cover both the watchman and leadership, the characteristics and roles of a watchman, and the responsibilities of both the leader and the watchman concerning the reports.)

Intercessors

The information God gives a watchman is never to be used for gossip. God entrusts to watchmen information concerning individuals or churches and that information should be treated as top secret from the General Himself! The very first thing one will need to do concerning the information is to pray! Remember how Abraham responded to the word that God gave him concerning the future of Sodom and Gomorrah (Gen. 18:17-32 discussed in c. 3). He immediately interceded on behalf of the people there. This should be our attitude as watchmen. We need to intercede on behalf of the situation that God has exposed to us. This is the sign of a maturing watchman. Many intercessors will be given watchman dreams or visions because God knows they are faithful to pray concerning the situations. One of our greatest attacks against the enemy is prayer.

> *Finally, my brethren, be strong in the Lord and in the power of his might. Put on the whole armor of God that you may be able to stand against the wiles of the devil. For we do not wrestle against flesh and blood, but against principalities, against powers, against the rulers of the darkness of this age, against spiritual hosts of wickedness in the heavenly places. Therefore take up the whole armor of God, that you may be able to withstand in the evil day, and having done all, to stand. Stand therefore, having girded your waist with truth, having put on the breastplate of righteousness, and having shod your feet with the preparation of the gospel of peace; above all, taking the shield of faith with which you will be able to quench all the fiery darts of the wicked one. And take the helmet of salvation, and the sword of the Spirit, which is the word of God; **praying always with all prayer and supplication in the Spirit, being watchful to this end with all***

perseverance and supplication for all the saints
(Ephesians 6:10-18).

We don't wrestle against flesh and blood; we wrestle against principalities, against powers, against the rulers of the darkness of this age, against spiritual hosts of wickedness in the heavenly places. We wrestle against Satan and his demons and our plan of attack comes through prayer and the Word of God! We can knock out many of the attacks through our faithfulness in prayer. "One can put a thousand to flight, but two can put ten thousand to flight!" If one can put a thousand to flight, then you have already begun to defuse the enemy forces when you start to pray. Then once you report what God has shown and incorporate the prayer of the other person or church members, you have increased your military forces and outnumber the enemy by masses!

We must also be careful as to how we report the dream. An immature watchman will report their dream in a panic, bringing confusion to the situation, whereas a maturing watchman will have had prayer go before him and know that God is "able to do exceedingly, abundantly more than we ask or think" (Ephesians 3:20). "Greater is He that is in us, than he that is in the world" (I John 4:4). "No weapon formed against us shall prosper" (Isaiah 54:17). When we get warnings in a dream, we have just seen the plan of attack or scheme of the enemy. God is exposing our enemy's tactics, which gives us an advantage. A good example of the immature watchmen vs. the mature watchman can be seen in Numbers 13.

> *Then Moses sent them to spy out the land of Canaan, and said to them, "Go up this way into the South, and go up to the mountains, and see what the land is like; whether the people who dwell in it are strong or weak, few or many;*

whether the land they dwell in is good or bad;
whether the cities they inhabit are like camps or
strongholds; whether the land is rich or poor; and
whether there are forests there or not. Be of good
courage. And bring some of the fruit of the land."
Now the time was the season of the first ripe
grapes. So they went up and spied out the land
from the Wilderness of Zin as far as Rehob, near
the entrance of Hamath. And they went up
through the South and acme to Hebron; Ahiman,
Sheshai, and Talmai, the descendants of Anak,
were there. (Now Hebron was built seven years
before Zoan in Egypt.) Then they came to the
Valley of Eshcol, and there cut down a branch
with one cluster of grapes, they carried it between
two of them on a pole. They also brought some of
the pomegranate and figs. This place was called
the Valley of Eshcol, because of the cluster which
the men of Israel cut down there. And they
returned from spying out the land after forty days.
Now they departed and came back to Moses and
Aaron and all the congregation of the children of
Israel in the Wilderness of Paran, at Kadesh; they
brought back word to them and to all the
congregation, and showed them the fruit of the
land. Then they told him and said; "We went to
the land where you sent us. It truly flows with
milk and honey, and this is its fruit. Nevertheless
the people who dwell in the land are strong; the
cities are fortified and very large; moreover we
saw the descendants of Anak there. The
Amalekites dwell in the land of the South; the
Hittites, the Jebusites, and the Amorites dwell in
the mountains; and the Canaanites dwell by the

sea and along the banks of the Jordan." Then Caleb quieted the people before Moses, and said, "Let us go up at once and take possession, for we are well able to overcome it." But the men who had gone up with him said, "We are not able to go up against the people, for they are stronger than we." And they gave the children of Israel a bad report of the land which they had spied out, saying, "The land through which we have gone as spies is a land that devours its inhabitants, and all the people whom we saw in it are men of great stature. There we saw the giants (the descendants of Anak came from the giants); and we were like grasshoppers in our own sight and so we were in their sight" (Numbers 13:17-33).

We see from these scriptures that the immature watchmen (spies) could only see the giants and reacted in despair, whereas Caleb (and Joshua, c. 14) knew they served a mighty God who was able to overcome the enemy, even though the enemy appeared to be giants. The immature watchman will see the problem without seeing God's power and will react with fear, whereas the mature watchman will behold God's power, have an overcoming attitude, and will not fear no matter how big the giant may be!

Chapter 7

Pizza Dreams

Just as you should not throw out your soul dreams, likewise you will not want to toss out a dream simply because you think it may be a "pizza dream." (I have yet to find a scripture that says our dreams can be caused by the food we eat!) Many people will refer to a dream as a "pizza dream" because they had been thinking about something earlier in the day and now it crops up in their dream, or because the dream seems outright bizarre, thus they chalk it up to the pizza or spicy food they ate the night before. But as we have seen, dreams can be bizarre. They can also concern matters we have thought about earlier. Just because we may have thought about certain things earlier, doesn't mean God couldn't have given the dream to us. There are times when we might have some of the busyness of our day pop up in our dreams, but I have found this to generally happen when I have been extremely tired or stressed for a period of time. Like all dreams, they should be examined and not tossed out just because we think it could be the busyness of our day that may have filtered into the dream. There are examples in scripture of an individual pondering about a situation and then having a dream related to their previous thoughts.

But when he (Joseph) heard that Archelaus was reigning over Judea instead of his father Herod, he was afraid to go there. And being warned by

> *God in a dream, he turned aside into the region of*
> *Galilee* (Matthew 2:22).

Joseph had been worrying about what King Archelaus, Herod's son, might do if Joseph were to return to Israel. Archelaus's father Herod had put to death all the children from two years old and under, which forced Joseph and his family to flee to Egypt in the first place. Joseph knew he was to return because an angel had told him so in a dream, yet on his way Joseph feared the outcome. God then warned Joseph in a dream to turn aside to the region of Galilee. Joseph could have attributed this dream to musing on it during that day, yet he was accustomed to God speaking to him through dreams, so he responded by turning aside to Galilee as God had instructed.

> *As for you, O king, **thoughts came to your mind**
> *while on your bed, about what would come to pass*
> *after this; and He who reveals secrets has made*
> *known to you what will be. But as for me, this*
> *secret has not been revealed to me because I have*
> *more wisdom than anyone living, but for our*
> *sakes who make known the interpretation to the*
> *king, and **that you may know the thoughts of***
> ***your heart*** (Daniel 2:29,20).

King Nebuchadnezzar had a dream which he was unable to interpret; he had ordered all the wise men and magicians to be killed if they were unable to tell him the dream and its interpretation. Daniel fasted and prayed and God revealed to him Nebuchadnezzar's dream. Based on what God showed him, Daniel tells the king that the dream was an answer to what he had been thinking about earlier that evening.

Is it Junk Mail?

We must be careful that we don't treat our dreams as junk mail. Once after returning from a ministry trip, I sorted through the waiting mail, tossing the junk mail into the garbage. I almost tossed out something very important because by the envelope it appeared to be junk mail. Thank God that I felt prompted instead to open it because inside there was an unexpected check for over nine hundred dollars. Likewise, you can toss out something important from your spiritual dreams by treating them as junk mail.

Once I had shopped without success on different days for the perfect purse. That night I dreamt about purses, but didn't give it much thought. The next two nights I again dreamt about purses and finally realized that God must be trying to give me a message. It turned out God was trying to speak to me about finances. I had been preparing to do a conference and was planning to rent a hotel, advertise, and absorb all the costs involved which were beyond what I had ever previously needed to do. Generally, when I would be invited to speak all my expenses would be paid for by the inviting church or ministry. When these dreams came, I had been fretting as to whether the ministry could handle such an expense. It took God a few days to get my attention because I had blamed the purse dreams on the busyness of my day. As I pondered my dreams, I realized that God had a very encouraging word for me as well as a slight rebuke!

In the first dream, I was driving along a mall when out of the corner of my eye I saw a person get knocked down and an assailant running away with a purse in his hand. I braked the car and rushed to the victim, a bald man. I tried to calm the man and told him I would be getting help, all the while trying to spot the assailant so I could describe him to the police. I called 911 as I handled the situation in a calm, rational manner unlike what I would do in the natural. Through this dream, God was showing me that the enemy was trying to steal the finances from the prophetic gifting by trying to keep me from doing my seminar. Men rarely carry purses so the bald victim was a prophetic symbol: Elisha was a bald prophet (II Kings chapter 2:23-24). God showed me that the bald man represented the prophetic and that the enemy didn't want me to present my seminar because it would increase others' understanding of the prophetic. By my lack of faith for financial provision, I was allowing the enemy to rob me. Of course I didn't have full understanding of that until I understood the next two dreams.

In the second dream, I was looking at some purses in a department store and found a small one not like what I had imagined, but I considered buying it because it looked so nice. Finally, I put the purse back because it was just too small. In the third dream, I was in another store where I spotted a purse that looked like what I had wanted but upon examination, I realized it was extremely large. The design was perfect but the size was huge, about two feet wide and a foot tall. Thinking "the purse was too big!" I put it back and woke up. As I pondered these two dreams, God spoke to me about my attitude concerning finances. I could believe God for more than the little purse (that is, small provision) but I was unable to believe Him for the larger one, thinking that was just too much money to have faith for. There was God's rebuke, but I was actually encouraged. The large purse had the design I wanted and could be mine, if I would simply trust God to meet the financial need. Well, I went on to present my seminar and God did provide the finances. Praise God! I am so glad I didn't toss those dreams away as if they were junk mail!

You may find yourself dreaming about something you did during the day or week. You may have been out looking at houses to buy or rent and now they appear in your dreams. God may be speaking to you about your spiritual house. Did the house in your dream need cleaning? Was it a house you would be proud to live in? Or perhaps you spent the last few days fishing and you dream that you have nearly caught a big fish, but it got away. God may be speaking to you about a person you could be witnessing to. He may desire for you to be that fisher of men. Whatever the dream content, examine it to make sure it isn't junk mail, or you may be tossing out a valuable piece of information.

Chapter 8

Double Dreams

Suppose you have had two dreams in the same night. This is not unusual; in fact, I can remember up to ten dreams in a given night though the typical for me is to have about three or four dreams. Sometimes these dreams deal with different subjects. The dreams I want to focus on in this chapter are "doubled dreams," that is, those with similar content.

> *Then it came to pass, at the end of two full years, that Pharaoh had a dream; and behold, he stood by the river. Suddenly there came up out of the river seven cows, fine looking and fat; and they fed in the meadow. Then behold, seven other cows came up after them out of the river, ugly and gaunt, and stood by the other cows on the bank of the river. And the ugly and gaunt cows ate up the seven fine looking and fat cows. So Pharaoh awoke.* **He slept and dreamed a second time***; and suddenly seven heads of grain came up on one stalk, plump and good. Then behold, seven thin heads, blighted by the east wind, sprang up after them. And the seven thin heads devoured the seven plump and full heads. So Pharaoh awoke, and indeed, it was a dream* (Genesis 41:1-7).

*"And **the dream was repeated to Pharaoh twice**
because the thing is established by God, and God
will shortly bring it to pass"* (Genesis 41:32).

Pharaoh had two dreams in the same night. Joseph was
brought to Pharaoh from prison to interpret their dreams. After
interpreting them, he explains that they were repeated because
God had already established the thing, and He would shortly
bring it to pass. Double dreams, those that have the same theme
or content in the same night, have been established by God and
will come to pass. When I became aware of this scripture, I
decided to test it by noting whether my doubled dreams actually
came to pass. Sure enough, I have found my double dreams to
truly be established by God and they do come to pass. The
"shortly" (Genesis 41:32) tends to vary. I have had doubled
dreams come to pass as early as the next day, whereas others
have taken a few years to be fulfilled. Of course, I still await the
fulfillment of some doubled dreams, yet at this point they haven't
been over three years old. I'm not guaranteeing that all doubled
dreams will come to pass within three years but I have found this
scripture to be true in my life, as well as in the lives of friends
who have experienced double dreams. Rather than my asserting
a deadline for a doubled dream, God will bring it to pass in His
timing.

God doubled my dreams concerning this book. He told me a
few years ago that I would be writing books, but I discounted it,
since I have never considered myself a writer. Less than six
months before starting this book, God gave me double dreams
concerning a book on dreams and interpretations. God
established that I would write this book and it is a reality!

God has fulfilled several double dreams that have been an
encouragement to me. However, not all double dreams are
necessarily satisfying to our hearts. I don't know why God
establishes some negative things as unchangeable, but He can as

seen in Genesis 41. Even though the interpretation of Pharaoh's dream contained bad news, Joseph was able to convey the wisdom of God to Pharaoh for a plan of preparation. Because of the divine wisdom, Egypt endured the season of difficulty. If you receive a discouraging word through a doubled dream, ask God to give you the wisdom and grace to handle the situation. God can turn your lemons into lemonade if you will let Him.

Whatever might come in your doubled dreams, God has established the thing he has revealed to you and will "shortly" bring it to pass. However, we must be careful how we interpret these dreams or we may be waiting for the wrong thing. I once had doubled dreams of a friend moving next to us on the same property. Before these dreams, there appeared to be a number of signs indicating such a move would take place. The double dreams made me sure of it. However, this family did not move onto property with us. When these dreams were correctly interpreted, though, we did witness a joining together. The dreams had a spiritual meaning established by God and came to pass. Instead of my friend moving onto the same property, she moved into a position spiritually which allows us to share the same location. It happened when we started Gloryhouse Fellowship that my husband and I pastor. My friend became the youth pastor and works along-side us! We had spent many months believing for these doubled dreams but with the wrong interpretation. I mistakenly viewed this dream in the natural, rather than the spiritual. We need to be very careful when we interpret dreams. In the next chapter, we will see how we can unlock the mysteries of our dreams and be less likely to misinterpret them as I did with these doubled dreams.

PART III:

UNDERSTANDING YOUR DREAMS

Chapter 9

Unlocking the Mystery of Your Dreams

This is what we have all been waiting for. How do we understand these surrealistic scenes which we call dreams? I hope to save you years of learning concerning dreams by sharing with you what the Holy Spirit has taught me. This is definitely not something you learn overnight. I have spent years and made many mistakes in learning to understand dreams. I want to help you avoid my mistakes. It's not that easy, though, to understand dreams and you will probably make plenty of mistakes, just as I have. Mistakes aren't necessarily bad; in fact, they can be a learning tool so the same errors aren't repeated. If God is speaking to you in your dreams, then for sure He wants you to understand them.

Where Do I Start?

God often speaks in parables and in a language that we don't understand. By analogy, babies quickly recognize the voice of their parents and will turn their head to hear mommy or daddy, yet they have no idea what the parents are saying. Likewise, we should recognize our Father's voice and turn our heads to hear Him talking. As babies mature, they understand and repeat certain words, such as baba, mama, dada, and one of their favorites, NO! As you learn the language of the Holy Spirit, you will begin to recognize your Father's voice as you discern which dreams appear to have come from Him and which have come from your soul. At first you might not comprehend very much, but as you grow you will begin to notice symbols reappearing in your dream like the child who hears different words and finally connects the words to the object. For instance, parents show their baby the bottle and say, "Bottle, bottle." Soon the baby realizes the word bottle goes with the object bottle. The more you "press through" your lack of understanding, the more understanding you will begin to have. Two-and-three year-olds generally have an understanding of our speech, yet they will still make verbal mistakes and tend to reverse word order or add what words they can in order to make their point. At two when my oldest son vomited for his first time, he explained, "I went poo-poo in the mouth!" Those were the only words he knew to convey his message. Likewise, even after a few years of learning the spiritual language of the Holy Spirit through dreams, you will make mistakes or misapply your understanding. Remember, toddlers do not get discouraged from learning our language and we must not get discouraged when learning the language of the Holy Spirit.

Joseph and Daniel were both dreamers and had the understanding of dreams. The Bible says Daniel "knew all interpretations of dreams, visions, and word sayings." Yet Daniel had to develop his accuracy. He lacked immediate understanding, as we will soon note. He had to learn and meditate, just as we need to. In Mark 4, Jesus speaks with His disciples concerning the mysteries of God.

> *And as soon as He was alone, those who were around Him, with the twelve apostles, began to ask Him about the parables. And He said to them,* **to you has been entrusted the mystery of the kingdom of God, that is, the secret counsels of God which are hidden from the ungodly;** *but for*

those outside of our circle everything becomes a parable, in order that they may indeed look and look but not see and perceive, and may hear and hear but not grasp and comprehend, lest haply they should turn again, and it (their willful rejection of the truth) should be forgiven them. And He said to them, Do you not discern and understand this parable? How then is it possible for you to discern and understand all the parables? (Mark 4:10-13 AMP).

Things are hidden temporarily only as a means to revelation. **For there is nothing hidden except to be revealed, nor is anything temporarily kept secret except in order that it may be made known.** *If any man has ears to hear, let him be* **listening** *and let him* **perceive** *and* **comprehend.** *And He said to them, be careful what you are hearing.* **The measure of thought and study you give to the truth you hear will be the measure of virtue and knowledge that comes back to you and more besides will be given to you who hear** (Mark 4:22-25 AMP).

There are no formulas for the dream language. If there were, then we wouldn't need the Holy Spirit. Jesus told His disciples that the mystery of the kingdom had been entrusted to them. He also said "there is nothing hidden except to be revealed." A person must be listening to perceive and comprehend that which is secret. He also said that the measure of thought and study given to the truth would be the measure of knowledge that would come back and more besides! If we want to receive more knowledge and understanding of our dreams, then we will need to give much thought and study to our dreams. God could have made it easy for us by speaking plainly, but He chose not to. I believe it is because He wanted to keep the secret councils from the ungodly. God spoke in parables so that those who earnestly wanted to hear Him would strive for understanding. He spoke parables, a symbolic language, both in the Old Testament as well as in the New. Since the mysteries have been entrusted to us, we must "press in" to understand our dreams.

Tools to Help

There are tools to help unlock the mysteries of our dreams. Each tool is very important and can help you to understand your dreams.

One of the first steps to take when you have a dream is to write it down. You need to write them down whether or not they make sense. Most of the time you will not understand them and while you are first learning you should still record even those dreams that appear to be from your soul.

> *In the first year of Belshazzar king of Babylon, Daniel had a dream and visions of his head while on his bed. Then **he wrote down the dream**, telling the main facts* (Daniel 7:1).

One of the most important reasons you should record your dreams is otherwise you will most likely forget details. Even when I retell a dream and later go back to look at what I had journaled, I realize I omitted an important part of the dream. It takes discipline to take the time to write out your dreams. It is hard to do in the middle of the night when you are waking from a deep sleep. I keep a recorder under my pillow that I speak into and then transcribe it in the morning. It is surprising how many of the dreams on my recorder I have forgotten about or am even unaware that I dreamt. One of my friends keeps a pad of paper and pencil next to her bed and jots just a few select words to trigger her memory in the morning. This works well for her, but I find that my dreams aren't as easily remembered. Whichever you choose to do is good as long as you are writing down your dreams.

The Bible says if you can be trusted with the little, you can be trusted in much. It was amazing to me how much my dreams began to increase by my being faithful to writing them down. I increased from having dreams a couple times a week to having multiple dreams per night!

You may be tempted to disregard your dreams because they don't make any sense to you. They may seem like a hodgepodge of scenes without a theme. That's OK, because most dreams will not make sense at first.

> *But the natural man does not receive the things of the Spirit of God, for they are foolishness to him; nor can he know them, because they are spiritually discerned. But he who is spiritual judges all things, yet he himself is rightly judged by not one. For who has known the mind of the Lord that he may instruct Him? But we have the mind of Christ* (I Corinthians 2:15).

Our natural man wants to immediately toss away the dream because it seems foolish. We think of it as junk mail so into the recycle bin it goes! We need to be sure that we don't treat any of our dreams as junk mail lest we miss something very important, as I nearly did with that surprise check I mentioned in chapter 7.

> *"For My thoughts are not your thoughts, nor are your ways My ways," says the Lord. "For as the heavens are higher than the earth, so are My ways*

higher than your ways, and My thoughts than your thoughts" (Isaiah 55:8,9).

God has an infinite imagination and He never ceases to amaze me with the ways He conveys His messages to me. As you begin to understand your dreams, there is a new and exciting intimacy that takes place with God. I get so hungry for more, even if the presence of God is while I am sleeping. I love to hear from the Lord in the night seasons, so much so that I occasionally lie down for a nap just because I look forward to the next parable!

When you write down your dreams, you will want to record the emotions you felt in your dreams. This can be an important key toward understanding your dream. For instance, you may have a dream that a loved one died in a car crash, yet you felt no negative emotions in the dream. You awake and panic because you fear this person is going to die. The key to interpreting this dream is to understand your emotions. It is clear by the non-emotion in this dream that it has a spiritual meaning rather than natural. In this dream, the person crashes his or her own car which indicates doing things in the flesh and not by the Spirit. The person's death could represent death to the flesh. The dream thus has a good interpretation. We must be careful not to wrongly interpret our dreams. Understanding our emotions in a dream will help us to avoid the wrong interpretation.

I can remember praying about whether to add a few days to a ministry trip I was going on in order to attend a conference in the same area. (I don't like to do things that just seem good without being sure it is God's will.) God answered my prayer through a dream. In the dream, I was walking to my house while thinking that it was too late to change my airfare to extend my stay, but suddenly I realized there was time. At my house I climb through a window to enter so that I could call to make the airline changes. My husband is inside next to the window as I climb through. Then I awoke. As I pondered the dream, I wondered why I climbed through the window instead of using the door; I interpreted it as a closed door that meant I should not extend the trip. That evening as I was telling the dream and my interpretation to a friend she instead received the words, "window of opportunity." This certainly put a different slant on the dream. As we discussed our two interpretations, she reminded me of my teaching to examine the emotions in a dream. When I finally applied my own teaching (practice what you preach!), I realized that I hadn't thought I was doing anything wrong when I climbed through the window and as far as I knew that was the way of entry! At that point I realized I had made a mistake in my interpretation. I would have missed a tremendous blessing had I not extended my stay.

Additionally, when writing down your dreams, be sure to record the date of the dream. Dates can be very significant.

> *And it came to pass in the twelfth year, in the twelfth month, on the first day of the month, that the word of the Lord came to me, saying;* (Ezekiel 32:1).

The Old Testament prophets recorded the dates whenever they received a word from the Lord. They must have known the importance of dating these words. Since dreams can be words from God, it is important to note the time of your dreams. God may give you a prophetic word through a dream for a church, city or nation and because you have written it down and dated it, when the dream is fulfilled, it is validated to the recipients. Also, God will often give a series of dreams which you may not have initially understand, but months later upon reviewing them, you can look at the dates and realize it was a difficult time in your life in which God was giving wisdom and revelation to you about it.

After recording your dreams along with the emotions you felt and dating them, you should ask God for the interpretation.

> *"I came near to one of those who stood by, and*
> ***asked*** *him the truth of all this. So he told me and*
> *made known to me the interpretation of these*
> *things"* (Daniel 7:16).

Often we forget to ask God for the interpretation! Daniel had to ask in order to have the interpretation made known to him. This was how Daniel learned and was able to interpret dreams and visions. The Bible says to "ask and you shall receive." We need to ask God concerning our dreams. You may say to God, "What does this mean?" or "Why was I doing this or that?" God will begin to disclose things to you as you take the time to ask and meditate on your dream. God has blessed me with the gift of interpretation of dreams. I don't have the understanding to all dreams, yet the ones that I do understand come to me without any effort. Usually, I receive the interpretation of other people's dreams but I have to work towards understanding my own. For a long time, I wondered why some interpretations came as a "freebie," whereas understanding my own dreams took much time and effort. God wanted me to learn the tools I am sharing with you so that I would be able to teach them. I hadn't imagined at that time I would be presenting dream seminars or writing this book! Another question then was why He would let me interpret some people's dreams but not understand others. The Lord told me it was because He wanted them to come to Him, asking and seeking Him for the answer.

If we feel we haven't received a direct answer from the Lord about a dream, that shouldn't stop us from trying to understand it. We need to go beyond asking and begin to seek for our answers.

> *Then it happened, when I, Daniel, had seen the*
> *vision and **was seeking the meaning**, that*

> *suddenly there stood before me one having the appearance of a man* (Daniel 8:15).

Daniel had to seek out the meaning to his vision. We need to seek out the meaning to our dreams. There are a few things that you can do to toward seeking out the understanding to your dreams. I try to break down my dreams by symbols. God will use a symbolic language and we often can find understanding to those symbols from the Bible itself. So I first check my concordance for a matching symbol. An exhaustive concordance is preferable to the limited concordance at the back of a Bible. Many symbols that God uses can be found in the Word. You would be amazed at the symbols that you can find in the Bible. For example, in one dream I was watching TV, a blend of a game show and talk show. There was a large audience and the TV host announced, "And the winner is...JOY PARROTT." I stood dressed in a gown and beautiful jewelry as if I were at the Academy Awards! Then I practically staggered to the stage where I was seated. The announcer briefly interviewed me, then asked the audience, "Is this God or a tweed couch?" I could see that dispersed throughout the audience were some people wearing grand poobah hats (like the ones on Fred Flintstone). When I awoke, I never thought in a million years that I would find tweed couch in the Word, but I did! A scripture from the book of Esther refers to a couch woven of gold and silver. To me this spoke of tweed, since tweed is woven material of different colors. This couch was in the king's citadel, the place where he would abundantly serve the royal wine. God was speaking to me that He had brought me into the royal palace where He was serving me the new wine in abundance. The poobah hats represented the "religious spirits" who were intolerant of the flow of the Holy Spirit's new wine. This dream blessed me because I was able to find the symbolic answer through the scriptures.

Some symbols may have multiple scripture verses so it will take some time to read through and find the reference that pertains to your dream. When I have multiple scriptures, I read each reference to sense if one of them "jumps out" at me or flows with the rest of my dream. Then I read the passage surrounding the verse to hear what the Lord might be speaking to me. I have been so blessed on many occasions by hearing from God through His word.

Sometimes you will not find your dream symbol in a concordance, so next consult an unabridged dictionary, not a pocket-size one. Again, you will not find all the meanings unless you have access to a larger resource. I recommend Webster's College Dictionary because Noah Webster was a Christian and many of the meanings will be Christian-based. You should look up your symbol even if you think you already know the meaning. There are usually several definitions for each word. I once had a dream with this person wearing a wig. I felt I knew what the word "wig" meant — natural or synthetic hair woven into a cap. It seemed so obvious, but after looking up the word and finding another definition, I realized that I could have missed the interpretation to this dream if I had settled for my definition of wig. "Wig" in this application meant "judgment or severe scolding," which put a whole new slant on the dream. Upon re-examining my dream, I realized its flow or direction and had my interpretation. When there are several meanings to a word, do the same thing as with the concordance. Read each definition to see if one "bears witness" or feels like a fit. Between the concordance and dictionary, you should be able to understand parts of your dream.

Another useful tool is an encyclopedia set. You can glean much from a symbol by researching it in an encyclopedia. I once researched eagles to understand more about the prophetic since eagles often represent that. I was thankful I had done that because I had received a prophetic word from a man who said he had a vision of me wearing a monkey's head on a necklace. This could seem to be a disgusting thing with a bad meaning, but it wasn't. I knew from reading about eagles that they eat monkeys and that the largest monkey-eating eagles dwell in the Philippines. God had been prompting to me to minister in the Philippines so this word became a confirmation — all because I had read up about eagles in an encyclopedia.

When examining your dreams, look for a symbolic or spiritual meaning. Most dreams should not be taken literally. Ninety percent of my dreams are symbolic while only ten percent are literal or directly mean what was shown in the dream.

> *I have also spoken by the prophets, and have multiplied visions; I have given symbols through the witness of the prophets* (Hosea 12:10).

You will need to think symbolically. Develop a symbolic mental attitude or you may miss what God is saying. I first search for a symbolic meaning to my dream and then if I do not find one, I begin to think God may have spoken a literal word to me.

These tools should bring some insight to your dreams; however, sometimes we won't fully understand our dreams for some time. We need to search out, pray, ponder and wait upon God for the understanding.

> *"Whom will he teach knowledge? And whom will he make to understand the message? Those just weaned from milk? Those just drawn from the breasts? For precept must be upon precept, precept upon precept, line upon line, line upon line, **here a little, there a little**"* (Isaiah 28:9,10).

We may get one piece of the dream and need to wait for the next piece. It will come in time, here a little, there a little. You may find the understanding to parts of your dream during your normal Bible reading time or when you hear someone delivering a Christian message. This has happened to me on several occasions. I would be reading and discover a passage that paralleled what I had seen in my dream. For example, in a warning dream I had for a friend, she was in bed with a gigolo who then tried to seduce me but I resisted him. I knew this man was a gigolo because I had confronted him about it. I didn't understand this dream because I knew my friend would have nothing to do with a gigolo! Later in my Bible time I read Proverbs 6:23-25 which speaks about the evil woman with the flattering tongue whose beauty you shouldn't lust after in your heart. By inserting the gigolo in the role of the woman I had my interpretation. The dream warning was that a spirit of deception was trying to lure my friend. I spoke with her about this so her eyes would be opened to the truth.

All these tools are simply the beginning toward understanding your dreams. In the next chapter, we will explore in more detail other possibilities represented by your dreams.

Chapter 10

Symbolic Possibilities

Things aren't always as they first appear in your dreams even if you are able to make some sense out of them. I remember how excited I was when I would apply the tools from the last chapter and parts of my dreams would make sense. It took me quite a while to realize there was much more to interpreting dreams than what I had already been taught by the Holy Spirit. God uses symbolic language in dreams and I eventually realized the symbolism may extend beyond a specific object or person to a broader application.

Are You Sure?

One of my early mistakes was assuming that the person in my dream represented himself or herself. Not everyone in your dreams is the actual character portrayed. God will often use a person to represent someone else or to give you some insight as to what He is saying to you.

First of all, a person's name may be the key to understanding your dream. That happened in a dream I had concerning my son. At the time, I was praying about how to handle a matter with my son who was living at home yet was over eighteen. (It can be awkward for a parent when a child is old enough to make their own decisions yet still at home; I wanted to be sure that I handled

97

the situation with care.) God answered through an unusual dream which opened in my living room where my husband's friend Frank was seated. I happily said, "It's been a long time" and as I went to hug him he turned into my son and the dream ended. I thought perhaps God was saying that we should invite Frank for a visit, but that was not the interpretation. Instead God impressed upon me, "I want you to be frank with your son. Speak frankly to him." Wow! There was my answer! Frank didn't represent himself in the dream; it was his name that God wanted me to focus on. Because of Frank's name, I was able to go to my son in confidence and speak frankly with him. God is so creative! Who would have thought a name could have been so much help.

Another time when I had been traveling a lot and feeling a bit dismayed, God gave me a dream in which Brook Shields was my personal attendant. She was with me wherever I would go attending to my every need. There was never a time where she wasn't with me, even following me into the restroom! Upon waking, I knew it wasn't possible that Brook Shields would be working with me so I asked God for the dream's meaning. God said, "I have placed a shield round about you. Do not fear or be dismayed." God encouraged me again as He used a person's name to communicate His message.

A person's name may also represent another person with the same name. For instance, you may know several people named John. You may dream about your neighbor John, yet God may be speaking to you about your cousin John. It is important to review all the dream details to make sure that everything in the dream relates to the person represented. Generally there will be something in the dream that won't fit the dream character indicating he or she is merely representative.

I have a friend Kristy and a son named Chris. In a dream, I was driving my son's motor home. I was about to cross a bridge when the RV stopped and I pulled over to the shoulder before being trapped on the bridge. In reality, my son does not have RV, yet my friend Kristy has a beautiful trailer that is like a motor home. God used word play by using my son Chris when He was actually speaking about Kristy. We cannot limit the creativity of the Holy Spirit in our dreams.

Another possibility occurs when the dream person somehow resembles another person. Perhaps you have met a person who reminds you of another person. Many times I have said something like, "You remind me of so and so" or "You look just like a friend of mine." God may use the person you just met to represent your old friend or vice versa.

I had an old school friend whom I grew up with from elementary through high school. I dearly loved this friend who had a unique personality and often peppered her conversation with unusual idioms. A few years ago, I met a woman named Linda who reminded me so much of my high school friend. Linda and I have become very close. We serve on one another's ministry boards and Linda travels with me sometimes when I minister. I often hear the same idioms and quirky sayings from Linda that I did from my old friend. This brings back fond memories of the relationship I had with my old childhood friend. After a few months of traveling with Linda, God started giving me dreams of my old school friend. It took me a few dreams before I realized God wasn't referring to my old friend, but was speaking to me concerning Linda. In this case, my old friend represented my new friend.

In another situation, the dream person had the same occupation as my husband. I could have easily misinterpreted this dream. God used a man of the same occupation to speak to me concerning my husband. In the dream, I was fixing a meal for my husband's co-worker. I set the food before him because he didn't know how to cook, and if I didn't fix him a meal, he wouldn't eat very nutritiously. Now I could have examined that dream and thought God was telling me that I needed to prepare some meals for this man. The interpretation clue in the dream, though, was the fact that both this man and I were wearing identical shirts. Generally you don't wear the same shirt unless you are somehow bonded. I understood that God was speaking to me about my husband, not his co-worker. God spoke that unless I prepared meals for my husband before I left for a ministry trip, neither he nor my children would eat properly. After this dream, I prepared and froze meals for them to eat in my absence. This didn't work as well as I hoped, though, because upon returning home I would find most of the meals still in the freezer. In my absence, they had resorted to fast food! At least I was obedient to God by preparing nutritious meals! On the positive side, I didn't have to cook immediately upon returning home tired since I had meals prepared for the next several days.

In a dream, sometimes one family can represent another family. Once I had several dreams about a family close to ours. At first I did not realize God was using them to speak to me about our family. In this case, it was a family like ours in size that God used to represent our family. Had I not become aware of this, I may have thought this family had more areas of concern than they really did. God wanted to deal with different issues in our home, not theirs!

There are many possibilities to role reversing in dreams. I have had my daughter-in-law in dreams represent someone else whom I was mentoring. My latest grandchild has represented a new work in my ministry. My dad has represented Father God, and in some cases, my mother the Holy Spirit as the Comforter. The possibilities are endless. I have shared a few so you can get the idea of how it can work. God will often use the real people representing themselves, but you must study all the circumstances in the dream before you assume the people represented are themselves. God will help you do this. You especially need to be very cautious when the dream reveals a problem concerning an individual or family. You should not assume that the people are actually representing themselves in your dream, or you may miss a word God has for you specifically or even for another person. I missed it quite often when I was first learning and mistakenly assumed others were having personal problems when God was actually wanting to correct some of my behavior. God usually will deal with you first before showing you others' needs. Remember when you see something negative in a dream, you need to pray for the person or situation rather than criticize or gossip about the information you were given.

One of the strangest experiences I have ever had in my dreams was when my mind and emotions were clothed in a different body! The first time this happened I was a little boy in the dream. I looked like a little boy, I felt like one, and I experienced all the emotions this little boy would feel. Nothing in the dream was familiar to me, yet it felt familiar to the boy who represented me. I was the little boy outside a home, near the family car while my parents were fighting. My dad was very angry. I remember wanting to bring my cat into the car with me but my dad wouldn't let me, and instead he threw it in the trunk with all these chemical compounds. I was worried about my cat. The fighting between my parents worsened and my dad hit my mother. I was very afraid, so I ran as fast as I could to an empty barn nearby. I ran to the back of the barn, which was pitch black. There I huddled grasping my legs in terrible fear and panic. It felt like I had been there for hours before deciding to find out if everything had settled down. It seemed so quiet. I was afraid as I slowly walked back to the house. There I saw a policeman talking with someone. I asked where my dad was and they said they took him away several hours ago. Upon awakening, I had no understanding of this dream. All I knew was that it seemed real. I knew it was me, but I am not a little boy! What could this mean? I stored that dream on a shelf for awhile until my second dream came in which again I was another character. I felt every emotion in this dream also, as if it were me. In this dream I was trapped in someone else's home where I was staying. I wanted to leave but they wouldn't let me. I crept down the hallway and downstairs to escape. When I heard noises, I ran to hide while waiting for an opportunity to get out. I felt trapped and bound by these people. After waking, I couldn't help but wonder again what kind of dream this was? It quickly brought me back to the little boy dream. I kept asking God, "What do these dreams mean?" A few days after the second dream I received a call from a woman in need of counseling. She mentioned something about living with people who didn't understand her. Suddenly I sensed that the second dream had something to do with her. She went on to say that every time she wanted to progress in her life, these people kept her in a "box." I asked, "Do you feel trapped? Are you feeling bound by these people?" She immediately responded, "Yes, you know exactly how I feel!" The only way this woman was able to receive anything from me was because God had paved the way by allowing me to experience her emotions. I effectively ministered to her because I truly understood her circumstances. Nobody else could understand what she was feeling because it appeared to everyone else that she had a perfect living arrangement being able to stay in this home with a kind family. Yet by the Spirit of God, I was able to experience what she was really feeling and thus able to minister to her. These people were holding her past against her and as a result she was feeling trapped and bound and was unable to progress.

Now I have had several occasions in which I have played the character of someone else and was thereby able to understand and minister at a higher level because I had experienced their situation. In one dream my husband was leaving me and I was trying to convince him that what some people were saying about me was false; yet he wouldn't believe me and left. I felt deep pain and loss. I also experienced the fear of what I would do now and how I would make ends meet. I wondered how my children were going to handle this. I felt every imaginable emotion that accompanies a situation like this. When I woke I nearly panicked. It felt so real that I wondered if God was showing me that my marriage was in trouble. It takes quite a while to compose oneself after a disturbing dream like that. Finally, I realized that it had nothing to do with me, but with a friend who was going through this very thing. I had been trying to minister to her for months but obviously was not meeting her need, so God had to give me this dream for me to experience the depth of her emotions. After this I was able to minister with more compassion and understanding. Praise God for the ability to speak by experience just how she felt. There is a saying, "If you walked a mile in my shoes, you would know how I feel." Well, God has allowed me to walk a mile in many people's shoes now. Not only have these dreams been words of knowledge concerning a situation, but also have been an effective tool to minister God's love and acceptance to others.

In another type of dream similar to these, I am myself in appearance but not in behavior. As an example, in one dream I was in my kitchen needing to do some baking and other errands. I felt pressure because of a time schedule. My family was present but they were not helping me. In fact, they seemed to be making matters worse for me by leaving messes in the kitchen and dining area. I spoke to my husband (who was a thinner version of himself) and sons about this, but they wouldn't listen. That made me so angry that I spoke abusively toward them. Even after telling my husband how stressed I was, he was no help. I became so enraged that I threw things at him even hitting him behind the head with the phone. He acted as though he wanted to physically fight back but he didn't. I was provoking him in this dream. I felt at my wit's end! I took some medicine and screamed, "I think I'm going crazy!" Then I fell backwards and my head landed against the sliding glass window. I awoke with my head shaking back and forth. This was a horrible dream. Here I was acting like a raving maniac! Immediately I asked, "Lord, do I have a spirit of rage and don't know it?" My behavior was worse than I had ever seen it, and I had thought I had been through more inner healing than this dream indicated. I realized within a few hours that this dream was not about me but for someone else. The clue was my husband being a much lighter version of himself. I realized, God was giving me a word of knowledge that another person needed deliverance from a spirit of rage. Praise God! Not only was it not me, but this person would soon be set free because of the word of knowledge. I don't believe this person acts this extreme, but God had magnified the dream so I would know what kind of spirit we were dealing with.

God will use unlimited symbolic possibilities to speak to you. Most of the dreams I have mentioned occurred as I progressed in my dream life. God was teaching me some of the many ways He will use our dreams for communicating to us. You may not experience these types of dreams to the depth that I have, but you will have a greater understanding of some of the ways God may speak. This information should help you, especially when you have found that certain dreams do not seem to parallel your life. I feel very blessed to be able to have such a wonderful dream life. It is somewhat like doing crossword puzzles or word search games, or even like putting together a jigsaw puzzle. There is a continual challenge which keeps me motivated to solve the puzzle. However, it seems that every time I feel I have come close to mastering dreams, God will bring me to another level which challenges me to understand even more. It seems that after every dream seminar I give, my dreams jump to a new level and I end up puzzled for weeks to understand them. This is how God has taught me concerning dreams. Even as I am writing this book, I have reached a new level that I have yet to understand. These new dreams are unlike any others, and as the Holy Spirit continues to teach me, I am sure He will bring me understanding and perhaps allow me to share the things I learn in another book. I'm grateful that He doesn't allow me to stay where I am at but keeps me always learning.

For Me or You?

When God starts to speak to you in your dreams, He probably will begin with symbols that are familiar to you. God gives each of us a unique symbolic dream language. What He uses to speak to me may not be the same thing He uses to speak to you. Perhaps one of the symbols that I have in a dream is a rose. That might bring back fond memories to you of hours working in the garden with your grandmother, picking the perfect roses for a table display. You can even smell the fragrance of the roses as you imagine them. Now to you the rose will symbolize a beautiful time in your life or at least something pleasant. But suppose my memory of roses is one of the thorns. Perhaps as a child I reached to pick a rose and was poked and scratched to the point of bleeding. Finally I throw the rose down in anger because of the pain it caused me. If this had really happened, then a rose would not symbolize pleasant thoughts to me. It would most likely cause me to think about the pain the rose had brought me, rather than the beauty of a rose. The point is what one symbol means to you may not be at all what it means to me. This is why we need to be careful about "putting God into a box" by supposing that each symbol always means the same thing.

There are many symbols from the Bible that will have both a positive and negative meaning. For example, a lion may represent the Lion of Judah, speaking of Jesus, or it could be speaking about our adversary the devil that "walks about like a roaring lion seeking whom he may devour." Likewise, a snake could have a positive or a negative meaning. When we think of a snake, generally we associate it with the cunning serpent from the Garden of Eden. Yet Moses was instructed by God to make a fiery serpent and set it on a pole, then when anyone who had been bitten by a serpent looked at it he would live. (Numbers 21). In this scripture the serpent had a positive meaning.

My mother's husband loves frogs. My children want to buy grandpa a frog on every special occasion. This bothered me because I had considered frogs to be a negative symbol. It wasn't until I went to South Africa that I overcame this anti-frog attitude. I was in a Bible bookstore where I picked up a bracelet that spelled "F.R.O.G." meaning "Forever Rely On God." I would never again look at a frog the same way. I realized now that my mother's husband has many reminders to forever rely on God! God is so creative and will never allow us to rely on formulas or limited thinking. He wants us ever growing and learning. He will continue to challenge us till the day we go to be with Him.

God will use things that are familiar to you as He speaks to you in your own spiritual language. If you are a doctor, He will speak to you in medical terms. If you are a mechanic, He will speak about engines and transmissions to convey His message. Whatever natural area you may have great understanding in, God will use that to bring forth spiritual meaning. He will also use your past jobs, where you lived growing up, the schools you went to and so forth. He will draw from your past things that were familiar to you to speak a symbolic message. I remember a few dreams I had that were set in an area near where I grew up, the city of Federal Way. It took me three dreams to finally get the message. After the third dream, I asked myself, "Why am I in Federal Way in these dreams?" Suddenly I realized that God was telling me it was time to have my ministry licensed and legal with the government. I was to operate my ministry the federal way! What a creative way for God to speak His message. Sometimes when we just don't receive the interpretation, God will continue to show a portion of revelation until we understand.

God may also use dreams to show you your spiritual condition. For instance, I mentioned my pregnancy dream in an earlier chapter, a dream that revealed my spiritual condition as pregnant with ministry. On the other hand, a different dream showed me that my spiritual state was not so good. Before this dream, I had been working on holding my own dream seminar. I had always been invited to churches or groups to present my dream seminar so all I had to do was show up and present my teaching. This time, I was on my own for everything from start to finish. Much work, preparation and money goes into hosting a seminar or conference. With no help to organize this seminar, I did much of the legwork myself. I had picked a date that was only six weeks out and that meant for a lot of scurrying to get everything done. I was driven to finish everything so my devotional time with God suffered. This took a toll on me spiritually, but I didn't realize that before this dream. In the dream, I told someone I wanted to get a laptop computer so I could accomplish more, especially when away from my computer. This person said my idea wouldn't work. "Why not?" I asked. She replied, "Because I had a laptop computer and when I started to video the bride (her "computer" was actually a camcorder) the batteries were dead because I had drained them on the bridesmaids. I thought, "She shouldn't have wasted all her time on the bridesmaids when the most important part is the bride!" This dream confused me until I pondered on it. I wondered how the computer turned into a video camera and what batteries had to do with any of it. Then God showed me that batteries represented my energies which I had used on the bridesmaids, instead of the main attraction, the bride. The computer is representative of my mind, and the camcorder the dreams or visions. Thus the very topic I would be speaking on. The bridesmaids represented my preparation for the dream seminar, and the bride represented those who would come to hear it. I quickly received this rebuke and changed my behavior so I wouldn't be so exhausted that I'd be ineffective in bringing the message on dreams to those attending the seminar! God showed me that my spiritual condition had declined because of missed time with Him. If I would keep my spiritual condition right, then the rest would fall in place. (Thank you Jesus for the message of grace!)

Important Things to Remember

As we venture forth and apply these truths, we need to ask ourselves several questions about a dream to help us understand it. The following questions serve that purpose.

1. What was the dream's subject?
2. What were the specific symbols?
3. What do these symbols mean to me?
4. Why did I say what I had said or acted the way I did?
5. Do these circumstances apply to me?
6. Do the people represented really represent themselves?
7. Does their name mean anything to me?
8. Does this person remind me of someone else?
9. Is there a message in this dream for me?

You may find that you receive some revelation or understanding concerning your dreams after these probing questions. From there you will have to determine the timing of your "word." Many times a message brought through a dream can feel like a "now" word, when it is actually for later. If you feel like God has given you a directional word, then you will want God to confirm it and reveal the timing. Many of my words have felt like NOW words, yet they were not, so I ended up making mistakes. I have learned that many of my dreams are for a future time. Knowing the timing is crucial. If we step out and do something ahead of time, we may end up falling into deep waters! (I've had my share of those deep waters.) Sometimes a situation in a dream does not seem to apply to you, yet God has not shown you that it fits with anyone else either. This could mean that it is a future situation that He is preparing you for. Keep yourself open allowing the Holy Spirit to continually shed light on it.

Beware of Wrong Interpretations

It takes time to understand the spiritual language God has given you. As a child grows, so do we. You will grow in your understanding as you seek God for answers and apply the truths in this book. You will begin to see which of your interpretations fit and which do not. I like to say, "If the shoe fits, then receive that interpretation, but if it doesn't then wait for more understanding."

Be careful of someone else's pat answers for your dreams. If you know someone is gifted in the interpretation of dreams and has consistently given correct interpretations, then I would give credence to their interpretation; however, there are many people who practice the dangerous New Age approaches and that are quick to give an interpretation. I repeat, you be the guide. Ask yourself, "Does it feel right?"

Recently I had a warning dream about false interpretations. In this dream, I was in a home talking with a friend. She had a book in her hand about symbolic dream meanings. I asked her if I could see it. She resisted and I immediately knew by the Spirit that this book was New Age. I told her that we would need to pray against the defilement. At this point she became convicted and agreed with me. I then prayed against the defilement that had come from the book. The scene changed and I was in a car with her and some other people. I stated, "God is the creator and Satan is the counterfeiter. Since Satan cannot create our dreams, he tries to counterfeit our interpretations." Upon waking from this dream, I realized how great the attempt of the enemy is to bring deception concerning dreams. He cannot bring the deception directly through our dreams, but he does try to bring it through how our dreams are interpreted.

Shortly after I first realized that God had given me the gift of interpretation, I was out to lunch with others at a prophetic conference. Someone overheard me talking about a personal dream and my interpretation. The listening stranger joined in with a different interpretation that didn't bear witness with me. However, I was new to the prophetic and at interpreting dreams, whereas she seemed highly prophetic. So for days I questioned my interpretation until God showed me that I had not been wrong. I should have known that it was wrong when confusion set in, and by the fact that her interpretation just didn't feel right. Remember, people do make mistakes. If you feel like an interpretation is inaccurate then "put it on the shelf" and ask God to help you correctly understand it. God is faithful to help us grow in our understanding of dreams and their interpretations.

In Review

Before I close, I want to briefly review some of the truths shared in this book. God speaks in dreams. He may give words of knowledge, warnings, corrections, prophetic promises, direction, and future revelations. Not every dream is from God. Some may come from your soul. When interpreting dreams, remember to think symbolically. Most of what God speaks in dreams is symbolic. Be sure to look up your symbols in a concordance or dictionary. Remember that not every person in a dream always portrays himself or herself. God will use rhymes, puns, riddles, proverbs and almost anything imaginable to bring you His message. They are complex in nature but just like developing yourself in any skill or sport, you will have to invest the time. The more time and effort invested, the more you will see yourself developing in this area.

God is so incredibly awesome and our adventures in the night seasons keep us drawing unto Him for understanding them. We should not fear "pressing in" to receive understanding to our dreams. A whole new world of revelation for you and about God will unfold as you begin to seek Him. I am excited for you and what God has in store for you. I pray God will increase your understanding and draw you unto Him in ways you have never known before. I want to leave you with this one last thought.

> *I will both lie down in peace, and sleep; for You alone, O Lord, make me dwell in safety* (Psalm 4:8).

Peace and safety is what God gives us in our night seasons. If you still fear that Satan could be giving you dreams, I encourage you to meditate on this scripture. Jesus tells us in Matthew 7:11, "If you then, being evil, know how to give good gifts to your children, how much more will your Father who is in heaven give good things to those who ask Him!" As a parent, I do my best to teach my children to be aware of potential danger during the day and I do everything possible at night to ensure protection for them as they lie down to sleep. When my children were little, after locking the doors and windows, they would make me check under their beds and in their closets to make sure there was nothing lurking that could harm them in the night seasons. This helped them to rest assured that they were safe and could lie down in peace and safety. If I give this good gift to my children, how much more will our heavenly Father give us this gift. He wants us to lie down in peace and safety. Now, if after I leave the room, my children open their window, then they have decreased their chances of complete safety. It's the same with us. God does His part, and we must do our part by making sure that all our doors and windows are shut and locked. We do not want to open the door to Satan's influence by allowing things in our life that are against God, as was covered earlier.

It is not God's character to leave us unprotected when we are unable to do anything to help ourselves. During the daytime, God's guidance is ever-present for us and we also have the tools to defend us against attacks that may come from the enemy. However, when we lie down to sleep, we are without consciousness and are unable to fend for ourselves. It is not God's nature to leave us defenseless. We can open the door that allows entry for the influences of the enemy so it is our responsibility to do whatever we can to close the doors so that we may continue to sleep in peace and safety. Satan cannot give us dreams directly, but if we allow him, he can bring influences into our lives which will indirectly affect our dreams. So it is here that I will leave you and trust God to use the information provided in this book to penetrate your hearts and bring forth wonderful experiences through your night seasons. May God continue to mature you and speak to you through dreams.

If you would like more information
on additional materials
or would like to schedule
a ministry engagement
please contact:

Joy Parrott Ministries
35855 57th Ave. So.
Auburn, WA 98001
(253) 288-0574

www.joyparrott.com
Hisjoy@joyparrott.com

Please inquire about quantity discounts.

New Release

Now Available…

**"Watchman, Watchman,
What of the Night?"**

Written by

Best Selling Author

Joy Parrott